The Sun Shines Down

The Sun Shines Down

SANKHA GHOSH

Hawakal Publishers

Published by Hawakal Publishers, 185, Kali Temple Road, Nimta, Calcutta 700049, India.

Website: www.hawakal.com
Contact: info@hawakal.com

First edition (paperback): December, 2018

Printed and bound at *S. P. Communications,* Kolkata

Cover designed by Shreejit Guha

ISBN-13: 978-93-87883-41-3

Price: INR 250/- [USD 9.99]

With love to the three pillars of my life:
Maa, *Baba* and *Shree*.

Chapter 1

The day was stuffy from the morning itself. The sultry climate added with teasing humidity made it even more unbearable. The curious eyes for the last few days miserably failed to grab any forecast of a mere drizzle. In fact they were greeted with the news of death tolls for this avenging climate.

Junaid Ahmed was walking down the lane towards their chawl in the narrow by-lanes of old Bombay. The over-crowded city also seemed to be in slumber at this dead of the night. He was late today. *That man came so late in the garage. Damn!*

Working in a down town garage in a metro city comes with a perk to be hands-on with latest high-end premium cars. And, south Bombay was the place that's ahead of the rest of Mumbai if not rest of India. Junaid worked there in the garage. He was also preparing for the job of *State Service Commission* and appeared for it. It was an umbrella examination for the recruitment in different central government vacancies. The written examinations were based on the class that the applicants have applied for. The *Class A* included the best of the positions. He wanted to be an affluent. *Like that one who came with a BMW today!* And, Junaid aspired for that. *The best ones!* Raised in a single room in a chawl in the heartland of Mumbai– Junaid knew what poverty meant.

"You are the elder one. You have a lot of responsibility towards your ailing dad and your younger one too," his mother would tell. "And, to you?" Junaid would quip back. Junaid's father Salim Ahmed was a factory worker in the suburbs of Mumbai. In an accident, when Junaid was merely four years of age, Salim lost one of his legs. Though frailly compensated by a small amount of money, Salim was asked to leave. Salim Ahmed couldn't take the trauma being on a wheelchair and being without a job. He started spending his time drinking. From the meager accidental allowance that his factory gave, Salim spent them on his drinks. It was not very long after this, one morning, he was found dead on a busy footbridge of a Mumbai station. His body couldn't take the toll anymore. Faiz, his brother was merely three years old then. Junaid took up a job in a nearby garage to support his family. His mother started working as a dish-washer in a nearby restaurant. But he never forgot his bull's eye. *The State Service Commission.* He would study until four in the morning and get to work at six. And, he would work for the whole day waiting for the night to fall when he would rush to home and open his books. *Or the dreams.*

The exam went well. But that day after a month of his exam, he received a mysterious call from an unknown man. *The bastard.* On the other end, the voice was cold and firm. "Do you want to get the rank? Need one lakh rupees. Your rank will be guaranteed. Else, forget it." As Junaid heard this, he thought it to be a joke from a colony friend. *May be the stupid Pankaj is joking from his new Jio number.* But, the firmness in the voice was extremely uncanny. He was feeling uncomfortable.

One lakh! He had studied all his life for this and now he was being asked to bribe for his dream. *I wouldn't. I would complain it to Afzal bhai.* Their local MLA. *He would definitely escalate it and get the racket caught.*

Afzal Shaikh was the local MLA of the area. He was a strategic placement of the ruling party for this place owing to the inhabitation of mostly a single sect of people. *Religion is the softest corner of people.* And, Afzal Shaikh was smart enough to exploit that. He would mention his clichéd religious sentimental dialogues in each of his meeting and speeches thereby buying out their trusts and acknowledgments of being a *bhai* of that area. And, in a span of less than three years, Afzal won the local election and became their newest MLA. "It's always been there against us. We are the minorities." He told Junaid as he spoke to him about the mysterious phone call. "Little can we do about it." Junaid was still searching for that *Bhai* he heard speaking in the meetings. "You have been a nice boy. I know your mother too." Junaid was looking straight in his eyes. He was experiencing a strong emotion inside for the first time in his life. "I will make it seventy-five." Afzal spoke on. "It's the system." Junaid could sense his blood boiling. He could feel his eyes red. He stormed out of the place.

That was the longest day he passed. He had lost the purpose of his life. That day afternoon, when his brother Faiz handed over to him the lunchbox from his mother on his way to his college – he couldn't hold his tears back. He hugged him tight. Faiz's shoulder was a place where he could find solace. "What happened, Da?" Junaid restrained himself. *I can't break down! I can't break down!* He blabbered under his breath. "Nothing. Go to your college. And, remember one thing. Never bend down against the odds." Faiz nodded. He could not make sense of his brother's rant. But Junaid wondered. *It was the words he was not telling to his brother but to himself.*

Afternoons were a bit dull. That was the time when rarely any vehicles came by. There were two other mechanics other than Junaid in this garage. Amit and Israfil. Amit was mainly for the bikes and punctures. Israfil and Junaid were meant for cars. In the afternoons, Karim Chacha, the owner of the garage, normally didn't grudge if any one of them took a nap or a break for an hour or so. Junaid used to stay back in the garage may be with one of his books while Israfil would take a break once in a while and visit his girlfriend at a nearby chawl. *She would be alone today in her room,* he would say. And, he would be back in quarter to an hour or so. Amit would love to sleep by this time. *Lazy!* But that day, Karim Chacha went out for some work in town. Israfil and Amit were both chatting. The sultry summer noon had kept the shop mostly barren from the morning. Junaid walked out of the shop. He took an auto. *"Police station."*

That day, he stayed back till late in the garage. A BMW came for a headlight issue in the late hours. He had to fix it. The owner and his family were on their way to Lonavla for the long weekend. *It was a Friday!* As he locked the shop and walked down the lane, he overheard a few whispers and fast steps approaching. But his mind was somewhere else. *I have informed police. They told they would file the complaint tomorrow morning.* He stumbled over a roadside rock. *But Afzal Bhai was a scoundrel. He befooled us all.* He suddenly heard the steps nearing him. As he deemed to turn, he saw two or three people running towards him. But before could retract, they were too near. He felt a strong hit on the side of his head. He tried to shout. His voice drenched in the blood gushing out of his head. Dizzy, he felt a piercing pain. Pain was engulfing his whole body. Paralyzing his senses. His voice. He could still feel the shadowy creatures looking like human being surrounding him. He suddenly tried to open his eyes and stand up. He gave his last thrust for life. *I want to live.* But failed. And, he fell back. To the eternity of nothingness.

"It is the sixth mysterious death in a span of last three weeks. The city of Mumbai is going haywire in terms of security to its citizens." The news read. "The lifeless body of the young victim was traced from the tracks of the local railway. The initial suspect considers it as suicide." Faiz was looking at the body of his brother. Headless. The police was still to find the head of his brother to complete the identification. It was the same shirt he would wear almost every day to the garage. It was the same fingers that he would feed Faiz even a few years back. He was himself amazed that he was finding his eyes dry. The tears have taken a leave for the day. He was finding it dizzy. Difficult to stand. He would run to the garage once more to find his brother there working. He would hand over the lunchbox. All these are a nightmare. He would wake up soon. And, would find his brother in the garage. And, hugging him tight. And, telling him... Faiz got back to his senses.

"Come to the police station. Identify and take the body." They have found his head lying a mere hundred meters away in the bushes along the tracks of the line.

There were almost thousand people gathered near Gateway of India with candles in their hands that day. Some of them were carrying placards. The placards read "Where is Security?" or "Government Step Down!" The gathering consisted of mostly people of middle to upper bracket of age. As the media was covering the gathering – they catechized for the reason. "It is a civil protest. We, as a responsible citizen of Mumbai and also of the country, are holding a protest against the callousness of the government in handling the issues. There have been six mysterious deaths in the city and all of them were young and civil service examinees. Can't the government see and take steps? Why the police seem paralyzed? Is it wrong to smell fish here?" told Amrita Bhimani, a social activist in the gathering.

As the gathering moved from Gateway towards Mantralaya, they were joined by another big group of people coming from the Chowpatty area. And they both headed towards the Mantralaya.

As the same peaceful gatherings continued for weeks – there were three more deaths that happened in the city during this time. And, all but one of them was civil service applicants. That remaining one was an examiner of state civil services. And, the gatherings too garnered their strength. From being merely a gathering of a few thousands, the current rallies were more active. There were student forces that were mobilized to participate here. Their participation was binding them along. With street dramas being played, colorful placards with memes and cartoons and networking over social media – this protest spread like wildfire. And, among the gathering and rallies including the student forces and the civilians, there is one name that has become familiar. He seemed to be the one encouraging and actively moderating all these. He was also seen giving out short speeches once in a while in the rally. It's Faiz Ahmed.

Shreya Basu was standing in her sprawling office room, looking straight onto the road that passed by. There were people gathered outside cheering her name. They came to congratulate the new Chief Minister.

She turned her back towards the window – looked at the piled documents on her table. They all remained to be signed by her. Malik was sitting across the table.

She could hear people cheering her name outside. *This is the best feeling. When people cheer your name and applaud you for something they have loved. It overshadows the guilt of being wrong,* she wondered. *May be this is the magic of power. Of being powerful.*

On warning note, Malik told, "They will be bailed out today itself. Once out, he will be after us."

Taking a sip of a rare aromatic Oolong tea from her transparent cup, in her impeccable style, she snapped sharp at him with a steel smile. "Things are taken care of."

Chapter 2

Today, Mumbai, India

Shreya Basu tapped her desk impatiently with a Montblanc fountain pen. She had a meeting with the Police Commissioner regarding the handling of increasing crowds for the civil uproar in the city. *These gatherings started long back during the last few months of the incumbent government. It has now gained momentum and is demanding quick punishments for the culprits.* And, the situation needed to be handled with care. The Commissioner was late for their scheduled 12 o'clock meeting. And, if there was one thing that Shreya hated, it was being late.

Her only boss in her whole life, her father, an immaculate IAS officer named Binod Basu, had been a stickler for punctuality and it was a lesson that remained with Shreya throughout her career, her life. Shreya was born with a golden spoon in her mouth. The Basu family was one of the renowned families of Kolkata since long. They have inherited the *Zamindar* aura and all the glory even long after. Though most of the *Zamindars* of Bengal could not hold on to their glory – the Basus succeeded in maintaining their pomp and grandeur. Excellence was in their blood. It had almost become a trend in their family to study in England and it has been followed for generations.

And, when Shreya passed the tenth standard, Binod began preparations for her move to UK schools. Shreya's mother was not agreeing with him. "What is the need to send her so far? India is quite equipped now."

"It's not about that. It is our family tradition. We must follow that."

Shreya was enrolled in one of the best schools in London. And, she loved London. She grew up to be a woman nurtured in English culture with high etiquette. She was a brilliant student and an astounding beauty. The boys hanged around her looking out for dates. But Shreya was conscious. She was a daughter of an Indian bureaucrat. So, she needed to be reserved in her attitude.

It was sometime around the second semester during her first year of Masters in London that Shreya was asked to do an internship. As a student of economics Shreya was above average, if not astoundingly brilliant. So it wasn't too difficult a task for her to get into an internship. With reference from her professor, Shreya got her internship at a British construction company which has grabbed a vital project under the supervision of United Nations and World Bank to provide economically satisfying shelter to the down-trodden. The first country selected was Syria. And, the project started off as a PPP model (Private-Public -Partnership). Shreya worked on the viability of the project and researched on every ground to provide a cost-efficient living. This was the time she even felt necessity of such projects in the context of India. There were lakhs of homeless people in India. If such cost-efficient shelters with extremely basic amenities were provided, it would benefit a huge number of people. Though she didn't know if it would ever be possible, she deduced a proposal viable for her own country. Once she even told about it to her father also. Binoy Basu also felt proud. For the Basus had always been genius and the same had also been inherited by her daughter.

It was not long before Shreya bagged her masters in Economics with flying colours and soon she enrolled for doctorate. And, it was during this time, she met Adam Parker – tall, lanky, long blonde-haired with sharp features and bright green eyes. Parker was doing his post doctorate in the university and was in his early thirties. And at the first sight, she fell for him.

Adam Parker was a son of a billionaire in UK. With no goals and good brains – he had been engrossed in pursuing various courses since his younger days. Never in his life had he fought with anyone. Never in his life had anybody succeeded in making him angry. Adam Parker was a person with immense knowledge. His favorite pastime was frantically going through news on his Android tablet or listening to Pink Floyd. Shreya found him cute and very shortly they planned to meet. She went with him to his patent restaurant, Bench.

It was in a different class. It was expensive. The average age of the waiters must have been sixty, all of them dressed as if they have walked off the pages of a Charles Dickens' novel, in long black aprons and stiffly starched shirts. Everything about the place from the cut-glass accents ricocheting off the walls to the smell of polished woods, was too English.

The moment Shreya walked through the door for the first time, she knew two things.
The first was that she did not belong here and the second was that Adam Parker did.

Before they called for a serious relationship, Binod Basu, her father was detected with cancer. And, she had to return. It was not even seven days to her return, her father died. Shreya thought of returning to UK. But her family did not allow. After the demise of her father, her mother was alone. Though there were maids and cooks, her old mother needed care. And, it was evident from her eyes. Shreya stayed back. Once or twice she thought of calling Adam. But, she knew it was never going to happen. So, she called it off. It was tough to tame her mind. But, real life had always been tough.
As she was settling down in India, she started getting involved into social activities. And it was not long before she became a prominent socialite. And in one such social gathering, she came across Malik. Abdul Rashid Malik. A prominent name of Indian politics. He was a man in his early sixties. Retired as the Vice Chancellor at one of the major universities of India, he had an eminent and a royal persona. He had been with the Red Party for last thirty years and had been an active witness to the

rise and demise of his party. Dark. Mid-height. Sober and very, very intense eyes. Malik saw Shreya in the party and in next thirty seconds, he was talking to her sitting on a chair outside the hall in the garden.

"So, Ms. Basu. How do you like India?"
"I don't know India. I just know some people here. And, they are…" she just raised her hands "good, in a way."
"A country is known by its people. You know some people. So, it can be taken that …"
"Wait… Wait" she distracted him, looking at his eyes, "You mean these people represent India", she curled her lips for a sarcastic smile, "I heard you were once a minister"
"Do you want to be one?" Malik threw it straight and blunt.

There were some intensified silences in the gathering that followed in Shreya's head. No. it was not for the Jack Daniels – it was the thought. The thought of politics, the prospect of becoming a politician. Finally she broke the silence. "I don't know. I mean … do you think I can… I mean… It's such a huge democracy."

Malik sipped from his glass of scotch and with a faint smile, he told, "Democracy is the most overrated word in the English dictionary."

The next day, there was a meeting in the Delhi head quarter of the Red party. In the last election held one year back, the Reds lost in every single state and lost foothold at large. It was time for a revamp. They needed a breakthrough strategy. And, Malik had the strategy.

The very next week Shreya took a flight to Delhi. She was sitting in the vast conference room of the Red Party. And, opposite to her were Malik and Srinivasan. Srinivasan was a person in his eighties. He was the person who started the party of Reds in India in late sixties. A young Srinivasan, started a fight against the government with issues related to the environmental hazards inflicted by nonchalant deforestation. It not only brought him support from the animal-lovers and environment-aware people but also from the top-notch intellectuals. Eventually, the media took him seriously for the reason that many celebrities started supporting the reason. In the 80s, Srinivasan became a rave in India. He was a youth icon. And, his party expanded nationally which continued long till the time he fell ill. Out of media, there was no proper face to carry on the party. The party which started as major one-face hype suddenly got rudderless. People started to forget the presence of the Reds. There were brains. A lot many. But they lacked a face to revamp their existence.

"You know Shreya, Reds are a cause based party. We fight for causes." The humming voice of Srinivasan broke the long silence.

"Apparently, everybody says so." Shreya was nonchalant.

"I actually want The You in our front." Srini ignored the sarcasm

"What do you mean?"

Three weeks later Shreya was the news. The opponents fired upon her as a lady in her early thirties with a Louis Vitton designer handbag and haute Ray-Ban with a snobbish expression and an extremely appealing face with a creamy complexion was declared by the Reds as their spokesperson. But the news was hot and was selling.

The news anchors were stressing every minute detail of her attires and style statements in their prime time shows. In no time Shreya Basu was a household name. Men were mad to have a real glimpse of her and women were keen to unveil her wardrobe mystery and her accessory detail. She became a celebrity. And, not the Reds, Shreya was the news.

Anyway, Malik knew Reds were always a one man show.

It never took long for the opponents to judge their potent rival. They could sense that her moves were very minutely operated with sheer cleverness. And, they all knew the mastermind behind it. Shreya was a discovery for the television debates. She was spontaneous. She was humorous and informative. She talked numbers. And, the TRP of the shows she was present reached sky-high.

Her interviews splashed at the prime times at every national level channels. She was not comfortable with Hindi at first. But, with sincere training she got prudent not only in Hindi but also in other regional languages like Marathi, Gujarati, Telegu, Kannad, Tamil, Punjabi, Oriya and also some North east languages. She herself was a Bengali. So, she almost covered all regional languages and gave separate interviews in separate languages. With time she developed expertise in each language and her reach to common people competed with the regional leaders as well. And, every other party started smelling danger.

When Malik felt the need of rallies to be organized in different states for the meetings of Shreya – he felt the need of money. The contributors who had been contributing were falling short to the demand to organize the consecutive rallies in different states and cities. Srinivasan was worried for he knew if he missed the train this time – it will be over soon.

"Pressurize the contributors for more." Srini told Malik.

"Can't do that given our work for last 5-7 years had been negligible."

"Then?"

Malik was thinking hard with a smoke. He made a ring looking straight to the ceiling of the room. "Let's see."

Next morning Malik was in a meeting with Bunty Ahluwalia. He was the owner of a leading Indian accessories company with a specialty in shades. He was in business for last 20 years with sheer success.

"How much do you spend in promotion?" Malik asked him.

For the first time in her life Shreya wore an Indian branded shades in her first rally in Maharashtra. The next day media went crazy – "Shreya Got Indigenous" and there were details of the shades she wore along with prices and description in every newspaper front page.

There was a sudden surge of demand. And Bunty Alhuwalia was stunned to see the result. The same shades that Shreya sported in the rally was sold ten times in a month the total shades sold from him in last five years. It was bombastic. And, he paid a donation triple as asked by Malik.

Soon, at the Red office in Delhi, there were series of offers from various brands to be sported by Shreya. But Malik was reluctant. Things should not be diluted. At least at this stage.

"Madam. Police Commissioner has arrived."

Shreya's permanent private secretary, Robert D'costa, broke her reverie. Immaculate as ever in a shining white shirt and a neat black trouser with his hair smoothed flat against his scalp, Robert smelled faintly of his Old Spice after shave.

Shreya looked at her watch. "What about the time? My day just got squeezed."

"I know madam. This shouldn't take too long."

Chapter 3

The march of common people on the streets of the city was getting intense exponentially. What initially started off as some sporadic gatherings turned out to be a full-grown civil uproar. Not only had the common people, celebrities were also joining the rallies showing their support. Slowly, supports started pouring in from other corners of the country. Even student unions of various universities across the country were joining hands. There were memes made against the inefficiency of the government and the corruption involved in the *State Services Commission* exam organized by the state.

For years, it was almost a known fact that many of the seats of this exam which enabled a candidate for a state government job were being sold out. In a country which was suffering from high unemployment and boasted of the highest number of youths in the world – the government jobs were highly prized. There were allegations against the existing government to have horse-traded the seats openly. The vacancies of over twenty-three thousand seats were allegedly sold out this time. The news channels were broadcasting the scam as one of the biggest in the country of all time. There were calls made to several candidates asking for money. Not just phone calls, as per allegations many government offices were utilized to reach out to the candidates for money. Even police network was allegedly involved in this entire scam. The price varied from one lakh to one crore depending upon the financial status of the candidate. On the other side, there were inside sources who claimed that the number of vacancies were nearly thirty-three thousand. But the exam was scheduled for only twenty-three thousand candidates. And, there were already five thousand new faces who have joined their new jobs. It was still in obscurity how they were recruited. The protesters claimed it to be the biggest scam scaling up to nearly twenty thousand crores! The state government appointed a Special Investigation Team for proper and in-depth investigation. But the movement in the same was negligible. The case was in trials but there were hardly any witnesses or evidences that were present.

Faiz Ahmed, the brother of Junaid Ahmed, was already in news for some time. Though he always shied away from being in the highlight, Faiz used to create intelligent memes for the social media alongside good quotes for placards. *I want to avenge my brother's death. But, I don't know how!* His mother was in a mental shock since Junaid's death. She had to leave her job of a dishwasher. Their family was in a severe financial turmoil. Faiz used to receive a few donations from the common people protesting. And, it was all that was running their family. It was Afzal Bhai who came to their small chawl once. After taking a look at his mother, he sat on a stool and looked at Faiz. *The introvert guy seemed to be in deep trouble.* "Don't worry. I am there. We are here to support. Your mom will be fine. I will take care of her hospitalization and all." Faiz was staring down at the floor. "Just you need to do one small favor. Today, some news channels will come to your place. Tell them that Junaid was never preparing for the State Service Commission." This is the first time that Faiz looked at him. He could see a man standing behind Afzal bhai packing the books of Junaid. *They wouldn't leave a trace behind.* Afzal spoke again. "Look Faiz. You are young and bright. From my MLA fund, I will compensate for Junaid's loss. Your mom and you can survive well till you get a job. What has happened is really non-compensable, but you have to move on. Your mom too needs to keep going." He patted on Faiz's back. "You need to study well and work for the development of this area, right?" He smiled. "I will look into that you get one." He was gone.

Faiz felt hollow inside. His eyes were moist. He could hear his mom murmuring under her breath. He couldn't bring pills for her to sleep too. *Junaid was very close to her. She is finding it unbearable.* They didn't have even food. *Afzal bhai was right,* he though*t, we need to keep going.*

Anjum Gupta was driving his white Swift Dzire through the Freeway across Chembur. *I got the interview today. The young chap was just amazing. He told what is required.* He could smell a pungent smell inside his car. *Like a dead rat. It's irritating!*

Anjum Gupta was a news broadcaster from News 24, India. Considered to be one of the veterans in investigative journalism in the country, Anjum was after the scam for long. But this was the first time where he was finding it difficult to crack the case. There was hardly anyone who dared to open his mouth. Even if someone was convinced – either it was denied later or the person was found missing or dead. After one long year, he was able to find an interview which can evidently join the missing link and prove that the deaths and the Commission exam are related. *And, the kid will go to the court too.* Suddenly a truck hushed by him. He was drowsy. *How come it be? I am feeling like vomiting also.*

It has been a long long day for him. After covering the protest march, he rushed to the narrow by-lanes of Mahalaxmi to the chawl. He saw a guy sitting and an ailing lady murmuring something. He could overhear her voice. "My mother", the guy referred. "Ever since Junaid killed himself, she is in trauma." Anjum quipped back. "Killed himself! Has he told anything like that before to you, something suicidal?" Faiz stood up. His eyes moist. He tried raising his voice but what came out was a trembling sound. "He was not aspiring for State Service Commissions. Spare us." He was weeping. He was trying to hold his tear back but in vain. Anjum spoke. "You may or may not speak out. You have the rights. You may or may not want to see your brother's killers being punished. You have the rights. You may or may not support us for standing up for Junaid and many others like him. You have the rights." He stood up packing his stuffs inside bag. His face got firm. "But you don't have the right to frame a person's death as suicide for your own lack of guts or for your benefit, I would say." He frowned. "It is for people like you why the Junaids are killed." He could see the guy broke into wild tears. "Speak Up"

Now he had enough to frame Afzal and link him with it.

As he passed the freeway, he stopped near a *paan* shop and bought a bottle of water and lit a cigarette. *The pungent smell is making the head ache. Damn it!*

Next day morning, the dead body of journalist Anjum Gupta was discovered from his residence. His face was red and swollen. His mouth and throat was red. His body was sent for autopsy. The reports revealed marked respiratory irritation, denudation and excess water in lungs which eventually triggered a cardiac arrest leading to death.

That night Faiz couldn't sleep. What kept on haunting him was the headless body of Junaid on the tracks and his mother's murmur from the room beside. He told everything whatever he knew. But then he remembered Afzal bhai. *For Afzal bhai was a powerful man.*

The next day was gloomy from the morning. The sun seemed too tired to show its shine. The cloudy overboard was stalling. Faiz went out to the nearby chemist shop to buy medicines for his mom. It was seven in the morning. The streets were yet to be engulfed within the cacophony of the everyday murmurs. He could see the roadside hawkers performing their daily morning rituals before the day starts and a few washing their cars at a distance. What he didn't see was a white jeep snaking its way up towards him, following him from a distance. As he went past the Jacob Circle crossing towards their lane, he felt himself to be roughly pushed inside the vehicle. He was blindfolded and a hand covered his face with something that smelled different.

He woke up in a room with his hands tied at the back. Naked. He could see a few plain clothed men around him. Standing. As he tried clearing his dizzied view, he felt legs hitting him. Mercilesssly. He was hit hard on his head. His elbows were hit hard to get displaced. And, there were punches on his face till blood came oozing out like hell. They were hurling abuses at him and his family. His dizzied vision blurred to obscurity. And, as he was feeling numb, he suddenly felt a shattering blow on his groin. He could feel the blood. And, the breath. And, in seconds, it was all dark!

As he woke up again, he was made to sit roughly on a chair. Naked. Dripping blood. Swollen face. Broken hands and legs. In his blurring vision, he could see a man sitting on another chair in front of him.

"We are police." the words came drumming echoed on his already bruised ear-drum. He was in a trance.

The man kept some papers and asked him sign. For the first time, he realized that his hands were untied. "SIGN!" He stayed still. Two men came hurling abuses at him and forcefully got his hands to the paper and made him hold a pen. The main person waived and asked them to stop.

In next few moments came a sack. The sack was made to cover Faiz and they tucked the opening and rolled the sack. And, they started kicking. The session of incessant kicking continued for nearly half an hour till they were perspiring like animals and started running short of breath.

Panting, one of them screamed," Will you sign, motherfucker?" There was no response. "Bloody dickhead." The next moment, they were kicking the sack again.

In the next morning, when he was made to sit on the chair, Faiz was bleeding from everywhere. His ribs were fractured. His face was un-determinable. Swollen and bruised. He was given a few blank papers.

"You're a terrorist. And you know what happens to the mother when her terrorist son is being arrested and is not cooperating with police?"

He signed.

The Previous Day

As Anjum Gupta found his way to Faiz's place, he faced a challenge in parking his car. It was a busy road around the Jacob Circle area of Mahalaxmi of Mumbai. With the approaching race course, Haji Ali Dargah and Mahalaxmi temple around, the place would remain always busy. *How one could kill someone in this crowdy area, he thought.* As he was restlessly looking for a parking space, he suddenly heard a knock on his glass window.

"Boss 100 rupees for one hour parking. Exceeding one hour is 100 rupees again be it one minute or one hour." An extremely thin boy of hardly thirteen or fourteen years of age was making the deal.

"Where is the parking?"

The boy showed a garage on the opposite side of the road. As Anjum was feeling a bit confused on the proposal and the safety of the deal – "Sir, we are open 24/7 and 365 days. Complete security."

Anjum laughed out. "You got the deal boy." And he jumped out of the car. He saw the boy sat on the driver's seat and drove effortlessly to the other side and parked inside the garage. As he got out and showed him the keys, Anjum walked inside the narrow lane which led him to the small chawl of Faiz and his mother.

After merely half an hour, as he walked out of their chawl, at the same moment in the garage, a person approached the boy and handed him over a car freshener and asked the boy to replace the existing one with this. The boy could feel the pungent smell of the same. As he was about to say something, they both could see Anjum approaching from the lane. The unknown person handed him over a hundred rupee note and walked away.

Anjum, standing on the other side, waved his hand to get his car this side of the road. He would take the Expressway to his place. As the boy sat and replaced the air freshener, he could smell a peculiar bleaching smell from it. *"Fuck it!" he thought, "Who buys this shit?"*

As he stopped the car and got his bucks, Anjum took the driver's seat and zoomed away.

Little did the boy know he had placed the pouch of bleach with ammonia in a pack of freshener. Little did he know that he would be instrumental in killing one of the best and fearless journalists in the country.

As the car zoomed away with a turn from the circle, that unknown person who handed over the freshener was standing in a *paan* shop lighting a smoke. As the car passed, he dialed a number. The screen flashed *Afzal Bhai.*

"*Bhai*, it's done."

Afternoons were the time when Afzal Shaikh would love to spend in some action. With rest of the day being dedicated to his party and family, this was the time he would keep to himself, especially to test his stamina. With a tall and wide build, Afzal was a quite a man in his college days. Though he dropped out in the mid without completing the degree to pursue his interest in politics, Afzal continued his pleasure plays with the newbies of the college as well as with his existing links. As all whom Afzal managed to sleep with would indiscriminately hail his extreme stamina and machismo of his hairy fit body and wide shoulders – Afzal never failed to amaze one in bed. Even at forty, he would make a nineteen-year-old girl come thrice before he came back to back twice in four hours of time in the afternoon. And, he would rigorously follow his schedule like one going to a gymnasium. A person who never touched smoke or alcohol in his whole life had a single addiction which he enjoyed to the core – sex.

But that day was different. He refrained himself from going out. Even his wife seemed worried. He was sitting by the phone with twitched brows and was drinking water now and then.

It was a call last night after which he seemed disturbed. It was Inspector Gaitonde.

"We need to frame a character for the Hyderabad blast. We selected one."
"What do you mean?"
"Afzal bhai, it will eradicate two issues at the same time. You don't worry. Just arrange for a safe house."
Afzal arranged for a safe house in the Vasai area of the western suburbs of Mumbai.

He got back to his senses with a call on his mobile.
"Bhai, it's done."
As he hung up, he dialed another number.
"One is done. When to arrange the next?"
"Tomorrow morning. Keep a watch."

It was a cake walk for them as Faiz came out to take medicines in the morning. It was scantily crowded and very few onlookers. They easily pushed him inside and whammed towards Vasai. The safe house.

Torture was a part of his daily routine. His body was slowly creating resistance against pain. Amidst this inhuman routine of sack-hitting, boxing, incessant kicking and at times electric shocks, he was concerned about his mother. It was after the third day of his signatures that he was taken to custody of police in Vasai and from there he was deported to Delhi. Tihar. *He was too dangerous a terrorist to be kept in a local jail. And, the case he was convicted with was running in Delhi.*

He had several court hearings. He would wait for it since these were the only time he would see the day light. He could breathe air. He could see his mother.

More than the innumerable kicks on his face, more than the solitary confinement in a cold shabby cell, more than the dehumanized and hopeless situation and his court proceedings – it was the helplessness of his mother that would make him cry.

His mother would arrive before the court was opened. She would go to the typists outside. She would get the application typed for permission to meet Faiz in the lock up, to feed her son her self-cooked food. Armed with her application, she would make her way among the crowd to the court where her son's case would be heard. *To catch a glimpse of him. I can't bow down to the pressure. I am not an escapist. My smile must fill confidence in Faiz. He is still a kid.* And, she would stand straight with her hands against her chest in the court hearings. Her face never showed despair. She instilled confidence. With her chin high. She portrayed hope. She was no more a no-namer. She was no more Faiz's mother or Junaid's mother or Salim's wife. She was in herself a lady of respect. She was Saira Bano. A lady fighting for her own son's respect.

The court hearings were mostly attended by policemen who arrested him. The chief of that operation – the person who made Faiz sign was Pankaj Gaitonde. He was made to be an officer of Special Task Force to counter terrorism in the city. And, there were his colleagues.

With hardly being able to move or walk, Faiz was sent for treatment. Within a few months, he was walking normally. Though in solitary confinement, Tihar spared him the inhuman torture.

It was one summer afternoon after two years of constant hearings and confinement that he was taken to the Deep Chand Bandhu Hospital. He was allowed by the court to meet his mother.

She was lying on the bed. Looking bereaved. He knew she won't be there for too long. He knew it was for that only he was brought there to meet, perhaps for the very last time. Saira's eyes were filled with indescribable grief. She was looking at Faiz also knowing that this was the last time she was looking at her son in this life. She wasn't afraid of dying. It was just that their life suddenly became hell. It was her son killed with head apart. It was her younger one who was accused of planting bombs in Hyderabad. Her eyes were filled with tears of love. The droplet rolled off her plump cheeks as she saw her son being handcuffed and dragged away by policemen. They didn't talk. May be words were too heavy for such a moment.

Two days later Saira Bano breathed her last. And, Faiz lost his last pillar to live.

Chapter 4

The main banquet of Taj Palace in Mumbai was a madhouse. It was filled with noisy, chanting delegates from all over the country. There were no qualms about the Chief Ministerial candidate for the party. The star who has outshone all was Shreya Basu. Despite the fact that Shreya was from Bengal – it was Malik's conscious decision to contest her for Maharashtra.

"Maharashtra is the bastion of the ruling government. If we can hit it there – we will get the national attention", Malik told as Shreya and Srinivas contested his logic for fighting out in Maharashtra elections. "The incumbent Chief Minister, the leader of the opposition party, has a low credibility and is considered to be inept."

"Unless you join ISIS and declare that on a prime-time Television debate", Malik told her, "You're going to be the next Chief Minister of Maharashtra."

After her nomination, Shreya flew to New Delhi for a meeting at the Taj Mahal Hotel with Malik and several other influential members of the party. Present in the room was Mr. Naresh Rajput, the head of the second largest advertising agency in the country. Not only that, he co-owns three major news channels in India besides heading a Market Research Company based out of Pune. It was alleged that Rajput was one of the most important factors behind setting up the government in most of the states where he had network. And, Maharashtra was one of them. Not only lobbying,

Rajput could manufacture mass reaction through his ad agency creative, spreading words using the social media platform along with his news channels on broadcast media and his associates, the political parties would bet for him to be on their side blindly.

It was not so many years before that Naresh Rajput would have been found working in an IT firm. He was a Data Scientist working with a huge stream of raw data and making sense out of it. Rajput's father Rajiv Rajput was a scientist working in one of the most prestigious research organizations of India and his mother Nirmala Rajput was a Managing Director of a MNC. Nirmala Rajput's story of rising up the corporate ladder with steady and calculated steps was like folklore in the corporate industry. She eventually became one of the most influential company heads and had direct influence on the government for several major economic issues. It was said that Nirmala Rajput was one of the first private corporate heads who worked hand in hand with government on several projects slowly creating her own impact and influence.

Naresh Rajput was gifted with a brain that boasted of numbers. People even speculated him to be better than his father in numbers. He was extremely sharp and focused. It was only during his post-doctorate in Austria that he fell for Analytics. It was a booming segment. Rajput loved data. After completion of his post-doctorate, he was offered a position in one of the best Analytics companies in the world where he worked as a data scientist. But when he returned India hoping to set up his own analytics start-up, he found the lack of awareness of the subject. He started approaching many companies spreading awareness that how could it change the scenario completely. But hardly anybody bought it before he approached the opposition party during an election campaign in Kerala.

The opposition leader, Jesu Alexander was a person who meant business. "How can you help us?"

Naresh Rajput, aggressively sported a presentation that would lure even the saint of a person. He pointed out three specific regions of Kerala where Jesu's party had never won. It was a stronghold of their rivals. "I would make you win these three regions. Free of cost." Rajput knew he had won the game. "Just you have to campaign what I will tell you to align with your own party's objective."

Next few weeks were crazy. He had appointed people to collect data from every possible source. Data was collected from the restaurants about what foods they ate to what television serials they watched to what social networking sites they used and at what time. A month down and Naresh and his team had all relevant data. Now it was time for them influence their behavior utilizing the data. The campaign of Jesu was designed exclusively for this region based on the findings. He was supposed to only hit the areas which were the sweet spots of the people found in the analysis of Rajput. How much irrelevant it may sound, Jesu's speeches used to have the analogies from the popular television soaps or others based on the popular interest areas of the local people. Based on the feedbacks or responses, Rajput created advertisement feeds for social media. All advertisements were made algorithm-ready for the different social networking sites. So, as people opened their social networking pages, they would find their feeds being flooded by news on Jesu's party. With regular feeds and updates pushed into their smartphones, an immediate connection was made. Within a month or so, Rajput was successful in creating awareness and recognition of the party in people's mind. *It was time to convert that into business.*

By including the party candidate's name and their slogans to the feeds, the people were slowly converted into prospective voters of the party. And, even before the election, it became evident, much to the ruling party's astonishment, that Jesu Alexander played a smart game. And, for the first time, Jesu's party won these areas and he eventually became the Chief Minister of the state.

From that day onwards, Naresh Rajput never looked back. He became the kingmaker of the country. To enhance the influence on people he took over AND broadcast news channel. Apart from his daily chores, Naresh also started appearing on TV shows conducting important debates and covering important political moves.

Though have been accused of being biased by several, Naresh Rajput continued to be the media baron and political lobbyist anybody dared to challenge. With a fiery blend of mathematics and marketing, Rajput was in a word unstoppable.

"Can we afford him to be on board with us, Malik?" *Srinivas asked before confirming on Rajput.*
"I don't know. He just wanted support for his business once we're in power." Malik told Srinivas. "But we've no other way. He only agreed to be a part of this once we contest for Maharashtra. This is the last chance to save our party. And, we are cashing on the already damaged image of the incumbent for the ongoing Exam Commission scam there."
Srinivas didn't reply.
Malik said, "Rajput will be in charge of running the publicity end of your campaign, Shreya."

"Can't tell you how glad I am to be aboard," Naresh Rajput grinned, "You're going to be my fourth Chief Minister."

"Really?" Shreya didn't like the man.

"Let me fill you in on some of the game plan." Naresh Rajput started walking in the room, swinging an imaginary golf club as he walked. "We are going to saturate the state with television commercials, billboards and optimally use social networking sites like Instagram, Facebook and Twitter to build an image of you as the lady who can solve any problem. But it's not like a motherly figure close to the earth. It's going to be someone like a star – too beautiful, too shiny, out of reach but can light you up. You get it, Ms. CM?"

"Mr Rajput…Can you kindly stop calling me CM?"

Naresh Rajput laughed, "Sorry. Slip of the tongue. In my mind you're already on that seat. Believe me, I am quite sure that you're the person for the job. Otherwise, it was too risky a project. And, as you should know, I'm too rich to have to work for money."

Beware of those who say they're too rich to have to work for money, she thought.

"We know you're the one for the job – now we have to let people know it. If you'll take a look at these charts that I've prepared, I have broken down different regions of the state in different groups. We're going to send you to the key places where you have to press the flesh."

He leaned forward to Shreya's face and said earnestly, "Your personal self is going to be a big asset too. Magazines and Page3s will go crazy after you. We are going to merchandize you, Basu."

Shreya found herself beginning to get irritated. "Just how do you do that?"

"It's simple. You are a product and you need to sell. I will sell you. We -"

Shreya turned to Malik, "Can I see you alone?"

"Certainly," Malik turned to others and said, "Let's break for dinner. We have an arrangement at the restaurant area of the hotel for the same and meet back here at nine-thirty. We'll continue to discuss then."

When they were alone, Shreya said, "What the hell, Malik! He would turn the entire thing into a circus!"

"I know how you feel, Shreya," Malik said soothingly, "But Rajput gets results. When he said you're the fourth chief minister, he wasn't kidding. Every election in India has had an advertising agency masterminding the campaign. Whether you like it or not, a campaign needs salesmanship. Naresh Rajput and his team know the psychology of people. As distasteful as it may be, the reality is, if you want to be elected to any public office in the country, you need to do two things – first you need to sell yourself well and second you need to lobby well. And, Rajput manages both. He is the best in business in creating image."

"I just hate this. I am the real self. People too are responding to this real self positively. Why to create an image?" she was restlessly moving are eyes. "Why to create this ….. I just can't understand." She looked at him. Furious. "Is this why they call this a dirty alley?" she lit a smoke and inhaled a long puff seeming to cool her down, "I will only go ahead with my real self that I am in my real life."

Malik's eyes were intensifying with every word Shreya was speaking. *She's right! Why to create an image? Why to fake?*

As he spoke, "Be it politics or life, there is nothing real." Malik's voice was calming, "It's only the perception of the beholder that plays." He looked into her eyes. Straight. "And, when the beholder is public, it needs to be curated to the perfection. That's the part of the price you're going to have to pay" he walked over to Shreya and put an arm across her shoulder. "All you have to do is keep the objective in mind. Mantralaya, right? We're going to do everything we can do to get you there."

"Do we really need Naresh Rajput?"

"We need Naresh Rajput. In Indian politics, you can't move an inch without a lobbyist by your side. He will get you deals. And, trust me, Rajput is the best at it. Let me handle this. I'll keep him away from you as much as possible."

"Thanks, Malik."

The campaign began. It started with a few television spots and a few personal appearances in Mumbai and gradually grew bigger until it spanned the whole state. Wherever one went, there was Shreya Basu in living color. In every part of the state, she could be watched on every regional channel, heard on regional radio, seen on billboards. From speeches filled with promises of development to full-page ads on fronts of major newspapers to rampant social media content creation – Shreya was everywhere. She traversed the whole state – holding more than thirty rallies to woo voters.

"We are confident of our majority. People are fed up with coalition politics. They want to see strong leadership." said the state spokesperson for their party.

Naresh Rajput had a chart of plans ready for Shreya. Their main thrust was on the Golden Triangle area comprising Mumbai Metropolitan Region (MMR), Pune and Nashik. This is considered to be the most urbanized part of not just Maharashtra but of India. And, Shreya's influence on the urbanized area was higher multifold than any other. And, this triangle itself offers seventy-seven seats out of total two hundred eighty-eight in the whole of the state. Almost one-third of the total seats. And, this is the major non-Marathi votes that they may dwell upon. As Rajput said, "This is where we will only present her suave image."

In the Marathi dominated Thane-Konkan region, Rajput took a calculated move. He made Shreya speak only on their region's richness issues and how she will take the region to a national importance. As the opponents watch her speak they wonder why she was avoiding the Marathi bet. The strong bastion of the ruling party – they were quite sure with major people Marathi, anybody would be hardly able to crack it.

But with a political veteran and opposition's chief ministerial candidate Mr. Manoj Pawar, hailing from the area, western Maharashtra was a tough challenge for Shreya to crack. Rajput deduced a chart to simply woo the mostly urbanized area which comprised of Pune and adjoining Pimpri-Chinchwad area and Kohlapur.

"We just need to concentrate on these areas," Rajput told Malik.

"But in northern and Vidarbha area? Aren't we relying too much upon urban areas?" said Malik.

"For the North, I have a separate plan, Malik."

The northern side and the Vidarbha area have a different political sensitivity. Manoj Pawar's close ally Ajit Amrutkar hailed from this region. And, they have a strong base in the grass-root level. The zilla Parishads, Gram Panchayats, the Municipal Corporations and councils have all been under them for last two decades.

Rajput created an anti-incumbent sentiment here. With the two biggest onion-belts Pimpalgaon and Lasalgaon in the region, Rajput's curated campaigns directly hit out at the growing disenchantment of the onion farmers against the oppositions who mostly held the *mandis* under control. The campaign was to ignite the voters against the hoarders and with the same time promise to give them a fair price with a national-level window. Shreya won hearts there in her rallies.

Naresh Rajput on their way to a rally to Vidarbha confided to Shreya, "All you have to do is to hit the highlights. No need to discuss key issues in depth. We are selling the product and that's *you*."

On the evening two days prior to the big day, Malik was having a drink with Naresh Rajput at Taj Land's End just across the sea line of Bandra in Mumbai. Sipping the single malt, Malik said, "Thanks Naresh. When we first thought of fighting the election out here, it seemed impossible. We had only a few trade unions in hand, that too, in hands of our allies. We have no grass root level reach. And, we never fought elections like that ever. I was afraid for we curated Shreya's image very calculatedly. If she falters badly here, the whole party will again bog down. But it seems different now. Though I don't feel we will win the majority, still it will be a brave enough fight to showcase."

"Malik, I told you that day. I don't play anything I can't win. You may not have belief in your candidate, but I have trust on my brand. I can see her in *Mantralaya*." He picked up his drink and said, "Cheers."

As the Election Day arrived, there were huge police protections in place. There were a total of two hundred eighty-eight seats to fight upon. There were three major parties fighting upon other than a few independent candidates. On the day, despite a little drizzle, there was a seventy percent

49

turnout of the voters. In some areas, there were sporadic incidents of violence.

As it was drizzling outside, Malik was sitting with Shreya in his suite at the Taj. Zapping through the TV channels, Shreya asked, "I don't know but I never even delved into the issues of the state." She said, "Not even commented on the Exam Commission scam once."

Malik paced up the room to her, "You know one thing, Shreya. You can't pressurize on the same issue that people already know. That's predictable. All other parties are doing that. Negative promotion always comes back to you as a boomerang when in power. You need to show people their dreams."

"And to realize?" she told.

Malik looked out at the sea from the wide-paned window of the suite. He didn't respond. *Politics has always been the business of creating conviction among the masses for a better future without the knowledge or proper intent of delivering it.* Malik knew it well.

The poll count started 8 A.M. that day. The whole of broadcast media were war ready for the complete and detailed coverage of the results. It was not only for the fact that Maharashtra was an important state; it was also for the fact that this election would testify the credibility of brand Shreya Basu. It would testify if the hype around this suave and beautiful lady was a fad or not. On a broader perspective, this election would prove if

India on a whole was ready for a shift to a different mode of politics. Polished. Logical. Matured. If proven, the shift to the modern and more matured governance would be only a matter of time. And, with more than sixty years of independence, it's time we move out of clumsy political issues restricting overall growth of the economy and the country as a whole.

Given all these aspects, this was a Big Day for Indian politics. Within a few hours it was evident that Shreya was winning. As the total number of seats count to be two hundred and eighty-eight, the magic figure was one hundred forty five to win majority and create government.

By three thirty, the final result was out in the media. Shreya won 134, the second party, the one who was defending its seat, won a total of 120 with its allies and the third party won 35 seats.

By 4 o'clock in the afternoon, the incumbent party played a masterstroke – the chief minister Manoj Pawar called for unsolicited support to the third party. They even proposed the chief minister position to their leader Mahesh Shinde.

Rajput seemed a bit knocked out. He asked his media to run news coverage giving headlines that the single largest party should be given the chance to form government.

The incumbents and the third party created a post-poll alliance by 6 o'clock that day. It was an offer the third party they couldn't reject. They would form the government with Mahesh Shinde as the chief minister and the current ruling party of the party will play second-fiddle to them.

Malik was calling Rajput relentlessly. But the phones went unanswered. Shreya Basu has lost the election. *She wouldn't be forming the government. She won't be heading the Mantralaya. The game is over!*

The coalition party sent request to meet the Governor to seek permission to form the Government.

Rajput picked up his phone. "Run the news in channels and state that Governor should ask for the coalition to form government."

He saw his mobile blinking. *Manoj Pawar was calling.*

The coalition party's leadership met the governor at his residence that day late evening. The Governor gave them a fifteen days' time to prove majority.

Both the parties would get a chance to prove majority. The coalition party was already claiming the same. However, Malik and Shreya would also get a chance to prove floor test at the Maharashtra Legislative Assembly or Vidhan Sabha.

The floor test to prove majority will be held fifteen days hence.

There was not a single comment from Shreya or Malik or from the leadership of the Reds. Their MLAs are all asked to keep themselves away from the media. *The party Think-tank would guide their stance. Would it be a setback?*

Late that night at around 12 o'clock, Malik was sitting on his couch with a peg of single malt in his hand. *He has avoided all media calls and even hasn't attended calls from Shreya or other MLAs. He only texted them to be silent for now. The party would let them know the future course. But did he know what his next step would be? Naresh Rajput wasn't picking up calls. The coalition government was forming the government. The dreams were shattered. The Shreya Basu brand would only be a theory or a Page 3 story.* He gulped down the drink bottoms up.

As he was asleep on his couch, on the wee hours of the day, he heard a beep on his number. *Naresh Rajput had a deal for him.*

Chapter 5

It was a closed-door meeting at the South Block of Raisina Hills in New Delhi. The PMO was buzzing with attendance of several Foreign Service officers, Defense Minister and a few other defense personnel. The Prime Minister has just returned from his tour at United Nations General Assembly in New York, USA where he has given out a memorable speech. His speech was one of the boldest ever by an Indian PM. Without mentioning the name of Pakistan, PM has hit it hard on the tyranny of Baloch people and even wished for their well-being. There was a clear hint that India would not like too much tyranny in the land of Balochistan.

"Welcome friends," PM entered the room with a spark of fresh energy even at midnight. "Need a go-through on our current border scenario."

"There have been a few ceasefire violations. And, as per our sources..."

PM cut in, he turned toward a person sitting beside the Defense Minister, "Any news from the facilities appointed in Baloch?"

The frail man to whom Mr. PM was talking was the Defense Intelligence chief of the country. It is a wing of the external intelligence of the country which works closely with the defense team to provide external reports of potential threats to the country. Under the able leadership of Kuldeep, the wing was closely working with the PMO and the

Defense Secretariat to confirm their stance on geopolitical issues and international relations. They were a key resource to help PM even take some aggressive stance on some occasions which eventually proved fruitful. Kuldeep Singh was a Military General and later became a member of Defense Intelligence's covert operating unit. He had been to Pakistan several times and knew their map like his palm. Owing to his common man look and frail un-distinguishable feature, Kuldeep Singh was hard to notice. But with his zeal and dedication, he slowly came up to become the head of the wing. PM was in constant contact with him to confirm their stance regarding Balochistan. But owing to the turbulent international politics, he wanted to play it in a different way.

"Post someone in covert with the nationalist people there. I want to make them feel that we are with them." PM looked around the people present in the room. "And, it's high time that we brave ourselves ahead a bit towards showing our power."

There was a complete silence in the room. Kuldeep said, "It's extremely sensitive. Pakistan monitors every little incident in this zone. Even a small hint can backfire."

Defense Minister looked up to the PM, "With the UN project in the Kalat area, China will be also investing in the CPEC… I mean in China-Pakistan Economic Corridor. So, not only Pakistan, we have to consider the other country too. Any intervention can be dangerous on that front too."

"Baloch is a rich and resourceful area. Even Afghans are after it." said Kuldeep.

Mr. PM looked straight to Kuldeep. "I want to post a covert at Kalat for the recent developments there. Their nationalist movement should also get a force." He continued, "I got a call from the Khanate of Kalat", he paused. "Even in this propaganda war, there is a human aspect."

After the meeting ended in the wee hours of the day, Kuldeep was helping himself with a cup of coffee at the Defense Intelligence headquarters of New Delhi. The analysis of the amount of risk involved in putting in a covert in such a sensitive area is time consuming. *And, damn, he didn't have time!*

The dawns of Delhi had always been blissful. Ever since he moved to this capital city of India, the hoopla of this city has been successful in keeping him away from a dreadful past of his. Even today after a long decade of the incident he could still see the same scene as he closed his eyes. Time has draped him in restraint now. He could now control his emotion. *His tears. Even when as he could see his wife and their three-year child's collected body parts in a morgue of Hyderabad, he would restrain himself. He was in a trance. He could see but couldn't feel anything. His sensory nerves refused to react. It happened on their way home after visiting her parents. Sneha, his wife, was returning from Hyderabad. On her way only, she halted at the Dilsukhnagar bus stand that a bomb exploded and lost her life along with Romit, his three-year-old son. The police later noted that Improvised Explosive Devices were used to cause these serial blasts in Hyderabad.*

Time heals all wounds. And time did heal up a lot of things. But, Kuldeep's mind never healed ever since. He lived with the tears. *Dried.* Their memories. There was no social life for him. So, as the Defense Secretary ordered for a special wing under Defense Intelligence specially to monitor the sensitive areas to confirm on political stances of the country, Kuldeep did not hold back and expressed his interest. Eventually, he joined and in less than five years rose up to the leadership. He hated his time without work. But with the new PM and their extensive foreign strategy, Kuldeep had a reason to skip his sleeps. He could now avoid his past.

One such day as he was moving across the office of Defense Intelligence desks, he came across a file kept on one of his junior's desk. *Hard Copy in the time of digital!* He casually took the file in his hands and was just zapping through the reports. The file name read: *Faiz Ahmed.*

As Kuldeep reached the Prisons Headquarter at the Lajwanti Garden Chowk, Tihar, he was greeted by the Jail Superintendent at the Main Gate. He was a person who defied all normalcies at any stage. He remained stoic to any wish or greeting. If anybody wished him, he would pose as if he never heard him. *Greetings and well-being are passé for him, he would think. He only meant one thing now. Business!*

"Where is the kid?" he asked the Super as he was making his way in among others.

"He is kept in a cell. These are the list of charges against him," Super told him and handed him over a paper.

As he entered the cell, he could see a tall, lanky guy of early twenties sitting with drooped shoulders. The cell was a solitary confinement. There were no rays of light. His entrance did not create any change in his position. He was also stoic to his surroundings.

"Kuldeep Singh."

No response.

The guy was looking down. Uncut long hair. Unkept beard. And, intense eyes. There was an air of innocence around him. *That's attractive.* The file wrote heinous crimes against him. It charged him with ten terror cases against him. They charged him for sedition and, also alleged his links to the *Hyderabad blasts of 2013*. That's what took him there. Though he knew that this file was nothing more than a crap, he was eager to see one who was framed as a result of the failure of the intelligence department.

"I know you're innocent and have no links to anything." Has he finished his last word, he heard a scream from the guy and he burst in to tears. As super was just entering assuming an alarm, Kuldeep waved him away.

The guy cried for long ten minutes. Loud and teary. And, Kuldeep didn't stop him. He could hear him say. *"They took it all. My brother. My mother." Kuldeep was not listening. He was trying to feel the agony so that he could even burst out once and can get rid out of his own past. Or ghosts. Or own self!*

"I know they have taken away everything you had. But now I want to give you something." The intense eyes were even intensifying with every word he was speaking. "I want your name to die and present you a life. A new life." Even before Faiz looked up to him, he was gone.

Two hours after he left, Faiz was informed, he had a court hearing next day.

Inspector Pankaj Gaitonde was a reckless person. Despite the allegations of his ruthlessness on the captives and fake encounters and his alleged closeness with several high-handed politicians – Gaitonde was a man of business. In any crisis of the government, Pankaj Gaitonde was the name to be called. He was a master window-dresser. With his immense experience and vast network and innumerable hooks around, Gaitonde was a man who could make things run or halt in the city. It was not him who maintained terms with the political honchos, but it was them only who wanted close allegiance to Gaitonde. And, Gaitonde enjoyed all the attention and power. But there was one thing that could easily buy him any time. *Money*.

It was not much time after his joining the police force he realized that it was not one's moral-superiority or bravery that fetch him fame and promotion. Rather it was another two qualities that were important. Brain and Money. It was the former that he owned and utilizing that - he garnered the second. And, with time, Gaitonde added the most sought-after third feather on his crown. Power.

It was on his first assigned investigation in the early 2000s in a sensitive area of Borivali in the western suburbs on Mumbai that he unearthed the mystery of a murder of a real estate tycoon and went to arrest the culprit who was backed by the ruling party. He was tipped off by an existing member of the ruling party for the same. As Gaitonde reached the plot, the police van was attacked by the mob. Gaitonde came out of it with a blank fire in the air dispersing the hostile mob and entered the spot. From the spot only, he dialed the local MLA and made a deal. *Seven Lacs to save the party name.* There was media coverage against the police inaction on the incident. Gaitonde was patient. In next two days, he kept a track of the criminals who were out on bail. And, he zeroed on one. That night, his house was raided and was killed in a fake encounter before the sunrise. The "Success" shone brightly on the front pages of almost all the dailies. And, Gaitonde was established as a powerhouse in the system. Hardly did he visited police station, there was hardly any senior even who dared to challenge him.

But this call was different. It was from Delhi Defense Intelligence. He was asked to be present before the intelligence team. He was told that he would be escorted from the airport to the destination the very next morning.

It was at the dead of the night that Baburam got a time of respite. It has been a long day. With more young chaps speeding on two wheelers, the number of unidentified bodies kept piling up every day. And, the age-old Sabzi Mandi Mortuary where Baburam had been working for last three decades has become a wholesome hell. With a capacity of a meager thirty bodies at a time, the mortuary had to accommodate over seventy. A reporter came today asking him about the *Dignity Of Deads* in the mortuary. He smirked and laughed loudly at his face. *Holy Fuck! Dignity of Death. Huh!* He was about to spit on that shitty mouth from where these words came out. *Dignity Of Deads.* But he controlled himself. There were camera and many other people who gathered in the morning. He got to hear that there were people who were protesting for that shitty concept of *Dignity Of Dead.* Baburam wondered on the concept. There were shooting innumerable questions to the in-charge of the mortuary.

"What about the bodies which were dumped, and we heard that they were not even properly stored?"

"Why have there been no new facilities introduced to accommodate more bodies?"

"What about the Dignity of the dead?"

With a bottle of country liquor gulping down his throat, Baburam was wondering what this "Dignity" was all about that all were concerned. There were piles of unidentified bodies lying there without anybody claiming them. After a period, rotten smell came out of those. Police were supposed to take them back in maximum three days. But they would hardly come by. And, those sheepishly stitched bodies with leaking thick blood and peeping organs lay there for months. And, all mortuary workers had to work amidst all this. Putrid odor of dead bodies has now been a part of their life. Baburam had developed a habit also. It didn't bother him anymore. Baburam wondered about those unidentified bodies that they were. Did those unclad, rotting bodies deserve more than a living body of him? As he gulped down the remaining from the bottle and stared up, he could see a fat, turbaned, Punjabi-looking person standing in front of him. He had two more bottles with him. Drunk to the brim, Baburam was too weak to stand up and stop him as he walked inside the mortuary. And, after the first gulp, he passed off with the open bottle in his hand.

As he was pulling two bodies wrapped in plastic out of the room in stretchers and were loading them in the van just parked at the gate, there were hardly anybody to take notice.

As the Punjabi-looking person started driving the van, he was slowly wearing off the turban, his false make ups and also the stuffed cotton which was used to make him look fat. As he parked the van at the basement of his Intelligence Headquarter, Kuldeep Singh breathed a sigh of relief. It was a long day. *And, tomorrow is going to be longer!*

As Faiz was getting ready for the court, he noticed Inspector Gaitonde sitting at the office of the Superintendent. Faiz started feeling the rise of temperature within him. He didn't know it was boiling of his own blood inside or not, but he started feeling the heat inside. It was hatred. Anger. That animalistic anger. His body was stiffened with rage without a venting hole. Far away, connecting with the CCTV camera of the Tihar office live, Kuldeep Singh was monitoring the movements of both of them.

"Are you sure what you're up to, Kuldeep?" the chief Secretary to Defense Minister asked.

"I am"

"But he is a novice and even doesn't have any training."

"If the mind is ready, physical training is just a formality."

Though not completely agreed with his views, the secretary to Defense Minister didn't get into any argument. Kuldeep Singh was known for his intuitions. And that, they never went wrong.

As the police van was heading towards the court, it was early in the day. Faiz was sitting at the back of the van, handcuffed, while Gaitonde was sitting at the front. As Faiz could smell a strong stench, he was feeling uncomfortable to seat. And, as the van screeched to a halt suddenly beside the highway, Gaitonde was going to ask the driver why they were halting midway. But before even he could complete, he felt a sharp blow on his head. By that time at the back, Faiz was already lying unconscious.

Their bodies were carried to a car waiting just behind their van beside the highway. And, as the car zoomed away with them, the police van started back on the highway. But now, it was moving with a reckless speed. There were only the driver and a guard in the van.

That evening, there was news everywhere regarding the accident of a police van. The driver and the guard were alive with minor injuries. The car was set ablaze as it hit a light post on its way losing the control over the brake. The two managed to jump off on the way. But the two inside the van, Inspector Gaitonde and Faiz Ahmed died in the accident. Traces of their body have been detected.

As Kuldeep watched the news coverage of the incident on his smartphone, he smiled at himself. He didn't know whose dead bodies were those that he managed to take out and place inside the van. *May be they would have been very good people in their lifetime and died as a shitty Gaitonde.* How does it matter?, he thought. The lifeless bodies. Little did they know that they gave life to somebody and would help to eradicate a junk from the society. Little did they know they are given the proper *dignity of the dead.*

The closed window room at the backyard of a farm house on the outskirts of Gurgaon was scantily guarded by two civil dressed intelligence officers. Inside, there were three people. Kuldeep Singh was waiting for Faiz Ahmed to get up. Splashing a bucket of water at him helped. As he woke up, he could hear Gaitonde's loud voice and sounds of kicks on the door. And, close to him, he could see Kuldeep Singh, standing.

"I promised to give you back your life. Now you have to promise me one thing."

"Anything you'd say. I owe it all to you."

Kuldeep Singh handed him over a gun and smiled. "See you outside. I am starting off the car."

As he walked out the farm house, he heard a sonic boom. And, then another. And, as he sat on the wheels to start, he would hear another three on a trot.

Inside the house, Faiz was watching as the bullets from his gun battering into the dead skull of Gaitonde exposing the pulp of a dead brain through a crack. Faiz was trembling. His lower jaw was shaking as if he was shivering with cold. He was breathing hard. The bloody body of Gaitonde was lying like a pulp in a pool of red blood. He fell on his knees. And, tried to shout out all his agonies. No voice came out. He was frenzied. But Faiz knew he had to pull this off. He enforced himself to cry loud.

And outside, Kuldeep heard a loud cry of an adult voice. An exhale of an enormous pain. This relieved Kuldeep off his own inner pains. His suppressed pains found a corridor of escape through another. As he could hear Faiz's voice shifting from loud long cries to weeps, he wondered how an act of violence gave way to an inner peace. *Did it?*

In another couple of minutes, he could see him come out of the house towards his car. Ruffled hair. Intense eyes. The exasperating setbacks of life with an engulfing array of pain and sorrow were released off him with the firing bullets.

But he was not Faiz Ahmed anymore for Faiz Ahmed died a few hours ago in an accident. The newborn was yet to be named.

The car zoomed away through the highway from Gurgaon towards Delhi leaving behind the gusts of a dreadful past. As Faiz looked up into the sky, there were the scudding clouds of hope across the zircon sky with the promise of survival.

The following few months were really tough. There was a rigorous training at various centers across the country. He was always being watched and monitored by the intelligence personnel. He was made to climb mountains; he was made to run miles under the sun and was made to live out in the chilling Himalayas with a river rafting schedule next day morning. Days were passed with excruciating schedules of training, but he didn't know why.

Once he met Kuldeep and asked, "Why am I undergoing these trainings?"

"Because you're unfit. And, you need training to perform."

"What performance do I have to do?"

Sipping water from his bottle, casually, he told. "You're going to be a mole for us."

Faiz stood as he watched Kuldeep walk away.

That night Faiz couldn't sleep. *Mole? Spy? For whom? For the system which brought him to this position? For the system that killed his brother and mother?* Faiz's eyes grew moist. He was panting. The excruciating pain of losing family was still raw. *How can I fight for this system?*

On the next occasion, as Faiz met Kuldeep, he thought of saying these. But he couldn't. But looking at his eyes, Kuldeep called him. After a few minutes, both were standing in a balcony overlooking the busy city of Mumbai.

"You know from the day when I last saw the battered body parts of Sneha and Romit's body in the morgue, I can't sleep. I can see only them as I close my eyes. I know there haven't been any accused arrested genuinely. I know the system has failed me in avenging my loss." Kuldeep was looking away from Faiz. His eyes dry. Voice firm. "But I still look out for them. I believe one day I will be able to find the culprits." His voice sulked. "But a culprit or two can't spoil the system. If we let ourselves fall prey to the lure of breaking it, we are following a bad example." He turned to Faiz and held him on his shoulders. "People like us have to come together to fight against these poisons to create a good precedent." Faiz was looking at him. Straight. "If we have a snake inside the house, it's prudent to kill it and burn it rather than burning the whole house." Curling his lips to a wry smile, Kuldeep told, "And, remember, it's not the house, that let the snake in. it's our negligence that it slipped inside."

The next training schedule was even more strenuous. Not only physically but it was also mentally exhausting. But Faiz liked exhaustion. It helped him overcome the haunting memories. He acted as a subordinate in an encounter case where he was made to shoot the first bullet. The power of taking lives was addictive but it didn't impact him much. *Emotions have all dried up.* From the first bullet he shot, his hands never shook.

After a successful stint of two other petty operations assigned to him, both in Kathmandu and the North Eastern frontier of India, Kuldeep was convinced about his progress.

And, next morning, they were sitting in the apartment of Kuldeep. It was time he would act on the Prime Minister's word to send a covert there. *And, he has found the one.*

Chapter 6

Kalat, Balochistan, Pakistan

It was one of those nights in the historical Kalat district of Balochistan. The smell of rose petals infused with the incense sticks sold outside one of the popular *Dargahs* made it a perfect setting for a *Sufi* night. A group of *Sufi* practitioners was in the middle of their show. The soulful music was both emoting and resonating with the crowd seemingly enchanted by the live melody. Out of the ten people on the dais, singing or playing any instrument, one seemed to be too disturbed to do any of them. Reluctantly, he was forcefully playing the harmonium with inquisitive eyes looking around suspiciously. But the colorful night with bright lights and colors all around overlooked that lanky figure among them. He could be effortlessly hidden as a non-playing reluctant junior team-member.

The Sufi night went on till late and once it was over while the nine people went inside the restaurant for dinner, the reluctant harmonium player left the place immediately and reached a garage in the next lane in a jiffy. He was supposed to meet Farhan Awuza in one of the local eateries. Farhan was a big fat man with eyes like popping balls and a weird beard which shaped like a Chaplin's moustache on his chin.

"Shed some bucks," he told in a rough grave voice.

"Here... Here"

Farhan handed him a driving license and identity proof.

The name read Hector Fernandez.

It was not easy for Hector to get lost in the crowd. His first thought after getting the identity cards was to understand what exactly he was supposed to do. *How can he help somebody fight the state? The concept itself is damn crazy.* He knew it was tough, very very tough if not impossible. He needed a hand to hold at the beginning and he knew none other than Farhan Awuza. And he decided to cling onto him before he got his feet stranded.

Farhan Awuza was a man of different colors. It changed with time. The more Hector saw him, the more he was amazed, if not stunned. He ran a crew of sixteen pick-pocketers and thieves in the city of Kalat. He was an owner of a garage primarily. It was a shabby, wet place where hardly any car ever came for repairing. Mostly, it was a place where other mechanics came looking for parts which they could not found because Farhan may have those from his pack of stolen goods or else he could get one stolen on request. He was a police informer. He used to inform police about the whereabouts of the local goons. As also at times he would inform the goons about the tentative operations and raids of police. It was a few days down that Hector understood well that it was almost impossible to decode Farhan Awuza. There were many foreign journalists who approached him to know about the secretive whereabouts. He would demand huge amount for leaking facts which were mostly incorrect even if he would know the correct information and would wink at Hector after getting cash.

"The news they ask are like something resembling the whereabouts of Osama. Or who have succeeded him. Even Indians come to know about Dawood's current location." He would light up a fag. "They also know that what I tell them is mere wild speculation. But they would buy that since everything packaged well, sells." He would pat on the back of Hector. "How about a primetime headline on a broadcast media stating 'Dawood is being arguably staying here' with a shaky handheld camera showing a closed gate of a big building." He winked. "It sells. People gulp these down with popcorn and evening coffee. Channels earn. I earn."

Hector could not decide what he would do to help him till he happened to meet Ghalib Alam, an uncle of Farhan.

Ghalib Alam owned a small travelling carnival. He was an extremely cheerful man. He knew astounding magic tricks. He started out as a street magician, joined a carnival and had taken it over when it went broke. Hector immediately saw his fortune. It lay with Alam. He decided to move with him.

Farhan instructed Hector to help his uncle run his carnival. "He is a man defending against the tyranny of the enemies. Help him in all the ways you can." Hector in actual couldn't find any relevance of his training and the act he was asked to do here. *How the hell can I help a circus err... a carnival party?* He wondered.

Alam was also in search of helping hands and a bright looking guy like Hector won him over. His experienced eyes spotted bright on Hector.

Hector was very fast to adapt it all. He quickly befriended the carnies. And, it was a world unto itself. There were "front-end" and "back-end" people. The front-end people were those who attracted people and coordinated with them. The back-end people operated the show. The most important thing to remember when in a carnival was that every minute detail is important and it's damn really important. Hector remembered Alam once said to him, "You can't con people unless they fell for greed."

The carnival had its share of nubile girls. They were fond of Hector. Hector was lean, sharp featured. His good looks were hard to resist for the carnie girls. And, in a few days, Hector started dating a pretty girl of the group. She was a contortionist. Her name was Soha.

Hector was trained in almost all carnival games. He was an expert in the "rat-hunt". It was a situation when a live rat was placed on a table. A bowl was placed on it. Around the perimeter of the table, there were ten holes. The game was if the bowl was opened the rat would run onto a hole. The holes were all numbered and bet upon by people.

"How could we gaff that? Do we need to train the rat?" he once asked Alam who started this game with Hector only.

"Put a little cider on your finger and touch the hole you want the mouse to run into." Alam winked.

In the next show, Hector acted a tourist and asked Soha to operate the game as per the cider-rule. He wanted to make it big that day. He accompanied a group of American tourists into the show.

"500 Pounds!" Hector shouted from the crowd. "I will go for 10th hole."

There were a few other participants. Americans were watching enthusiastically.

The rat went for the 10th one.

Soha in a pained face handed him over the amount.

"Rest girlie." told Hector. "I want to try my luck today. You have USD?"

"Yes. But, in that case if you lose, we need the same bet amount in return."

"Done."

The game began. Hector won thrice in a row. He received the money and walked off. One from the American group called up. "Hey, man" the big fat man was giggling "You are fabulous. Can we have a deal?"

"Ten percent mine."

"Sure"

Hector bet for a 1000 USD game. He won. And, the next 2000 USD. And, then he looked back to the Americans. "How much money you have now?"

"May be a 20,000 dollar."

"Take it out."

"If we win, we'll give 20,000 USD and if we lose you will give me 40,000 USD? What say, girlie?" Before even the Americans could react, the bowl was taken out and the rat this time went to a different hole.

The Americans found themselves surrounded by six hefty people for providing 20,000 USD. It was the biggest bet ever won by Alam's carnival group. By the time, the American group discovered that Hector was a member of the carnival itself by a poster outside, Hector was lying on his cozy bed at a town hotel and Soha was riding on him. That night, they made fierce love. They were all over the hotel room. They were on the table. They were on the floor. They were on the bath-tub. The strong hard masculinity was stuck with the delicate nobility spilling love everywhere.

During the next one year, Hector learnt a lot about human nature. He realized how easy it was to arouse greed in people and how gullible people could be. They believed incredible tales because their greed wants them to. With penny flowing in pocket and an aura of confidence, Hector Fernandes became someone who could be hardly ignored. He was confident in winning confidence of people. And, he knew, it was the biggest bet on the earth to win. He also knew that he was the best at it. He was fast to expert the art of changing make-ups. Ideas used to come rapidly. He could change like a chameleon in different make-ups. Hector also was good in mimicry. And in a very short while, Hector became an asset for Alam that anybody could afford to miss.

In between the carnivals, news used to come about Pakistani military oppressions on the Baloch people fighting for their rights and autonomy. One day, as the carnival was wrapping up, Hector was sitting with Alam. He asked, "Why are you fighting? Whom are you fighting? With such a meager arrangement, do you think you'd be able to get your rights and political autonomy for your state? …. And by winning a dice game or two I would be helping you to get that. Don't you find all these too silly?"

"It's not about rights and political autonomy only, my dear." Ghalib told Hector. "It's about your loyalty to your ethnicity. We receive hardly any help from anybody. There's hardly anybody who wishes to go against the federal government, but …" His voice faded.

Alam redeemed. His eyes bright. "We are the most prosperous state with humongous natural resources… Richest I'd say. We were promised autonomy. But never given one." Alam's voice were huskier. "We make 40 percent of the landmass of the country and we're given just nothing. Our land is exploited along with our people. Bugti was killed…" he paused, "They have all destroyed us." He showed a dry smile. "We don't have a common border with you… we wish we had one." Ghalib's eyes would shine in hope, "We are successfully resisting the injustice for years. Now many people are supporting us but still we need money to strive to put forth resistance." He coughed hard. "We will succeed someday."

"And, mind you young man, no resistance against oppression and exploitation is silly. It all runs in hope. Will. Belief. Even if you seem to be too small against your enemy, never lose hope. Continue your struggle. Victory will be yours. The Sun is bound to shine upon you. Else, there would have been no Vietnam." He patted on Hector's shoulder and walked away. As Hector watched him walk away he could faintly hear Ghalib humming a tune. *Bella Ciao ..!!*

In the next few months, Alam's health started giving up to the incessant hard work of carrying the entire carnival on his shoulders. With an ailing health, he was unable to travel with the carnival and consequently, the carnival team started losing the cohesive force. There was no one to take it forward. Hector went ahead with his learning from carnival days, and also Alam. This time, he thought, he would give it a try differently. He needed no-one but Soha with him to assist.

Few of the members working in the carnivals became the active members of the Baloch Nationalist movement that was staged against the government that time. The increasing corruption and oppression of the federal government resulted in a fiery protest which started as the mere demonstrations. But the mere demonstration resulted in arrest by the government and the police fired on the demonstrators throughout the country. And, the protest became armed. The supply of arms came from many secret parts of the world. But the rebels needed money. They needed money to buy arms. They needed money to run the revolution before it mellowed down to a mere up rise.

Hector's purpose of collecting money and catalyze the movement was becoming obscured. With the tyranny of army becoming rampant on the Baloch

Nationalist members and them going undercover, it was hard for Hector to do anything. Kuldeep Singh asked him to get out of the place. But how? There was absolutely nothing. Neither did he know how to get out of this place nor did Kuldeep.

Ghalib Alam called Hector in this time of turmoil once. After a few talks of old days, Alam asked,

"I have a good proposition for you. You get me some money." Alam's once-bright eyes have now turned to fade-green moist, "I bet you escape from here." He sat with a bit of his strength, "For the first time in my life, I see these people standing for a cause, for a very real cause." He paused. "I am not in a state to help them. But you can help me to help them."

Hector was staring at Alam's eyes. Alam read his mind. He smiled. "Alam never undervalues his own word."

That night after a hot session of lovemaking – Hector and Soha were lying on bed. The television in the room was running a news channel. They were both naked clung to each other – easing their body to relax.

"Can we even survive other than what we do – conning?" asked Soha, lighting a fag.

"You mean a different profession?" Hector asked.

Soha nodded. They both were pointlessly looking at the television where a news anchor was addressing some world issues in a fluent English language. They got back to their senses when they heard the word Syria from the anchor.

"... The United Nations project of providing shelter to every individual starts with Pakistani government kicking it off at the earliest in the Balochistan province which marks the China – Pakistan – Economic Corridor. The UN officials have already visited the place and had talks with the government here. The project will be in a PPP model where the private company will execute and the government i.e. public institutions will invest. This will provide jobs to more than 5000 Balochis, both skilled and non-skilled. The partner bank in this project will be Pakistan Global Bank. And, the British multinational construction company UBGC Corp will be executing the project. The main chief is Akhtar Ahmed Shaikh ... "

"How about being a banker?" Hector asked releasing a ring of smoke.

UBGC was a global construction company with headquarters in United Kingdom. They were prolific and acutely verified every minute detail before venturing into this new project. This time, though the project was approved by higher authority and has been associated with World Bank – they have made everything very clear from the beginning. It was a five hundred-million-dollar project. The initial payment has been done by the

Pakistani government – a cheque of one-hundred million dollars. Since Pakistan Global Bank was the banking partner – the money was kept in the account there. The fund will be utilized slowly with the progress of the project. It was a very initial stage – and the company was involved in wrapping up the final lines of planning.

Akhtar Ahmed Shaikh was appointed as the chief manager of the project. He was a man of barely forty in age. He was immaculate in his job. A workaholic by nature, Akhtar climbed up to this position of chief manager from almost nowhere. Though born in Pakistan, Akhtar moved to London when his parents relocated there for their jobs. He was studious in school. From the very beginning – he knew he was mediocre in brain but he made it sure to work on it to reach to the first position. He always gave the rank-holders a cold sweat in competition. He worked in other construction companies as a mechanical engineer after passing engineering before he was absorbed as a chief manager for this particular project by UBGC.

It was the second day in his new office. Akhtar was attending a conference call from his reporting manager at UK and their associates in Pakistan when he was given a visiting card by the guard.

"One person is waiting outside to meet you, sir."

The card read:

Murray Zaidi
Senior Manager
United Bank of Pakistan

It was two weeks after this day that Akhtar Ahmed and Murray Zaidi became quite an acquaintance. Zaidi became his only friend in this unknown country. And, Akhtar was quite enjoying this man's company. Zaidi was a man of knowledge. And, this was what knocked Akhtar off. *He has always been always fond of people with knowledge.* Zaidi had dark intense eyes and an athletic lean figure. Always updated on international issues and economics, Murray Zaidi had an aura hard to ignore.

At one of their meetings in the bar, Zaidi asked,

"Why are you keeping the whole fund in the current account? It never gives you interest. Instead you can get even more interest rate if you invest a bulk amount."

"They asked me to. But even I was thinking for doing for some high interest rate fixed deposits. How much on average is the rate here?"

"Depends. Any ways, I need to leave, Allen." Zaidi stood up. "I have some family meet today."

It was after another five days that Akhtar called Zaidi. After a few initial courtesy, Akhtar asked,

"Murray, tell me what rate is your bank providing for a term deposit of say hundred million USD? Or tell me a two more other bank rates also."

"Sure, Akhtar. I am on a leave now. Something personal showed up. I am asking a concerned person to get in touch with you and guide you in this regard. Please excuse me."

After nearly twenty minutes, Akhtar Ahmed's mobile was ringing. On the other side was a sweet female voice saying,

"Hello, sir, Zaidi sir asked me to call you. We can give 10.5 percentage of interest on that deposit. It's a call money deal for the bulk amount specially."

"Yes. Pakistan Global Bank is also providing that. But the issue with me is it will be necessary for me to partly withdraw the money at any time as and when the project requires, so they are charging premature penalty..."

"You can withdraw even the whole amount. We don't penalize you for this. But the interest rate in that case is 10.3. It can be done on Zaidi sir's recommendation and only if you can arrange hundred and fifty or more fund."

She also provided contacts of other banks. He didn't call them – he could see the rate chart of them from the internet only. *Zaidi's bank provided the best offer.* Akhtar mailed it to their senior about the details of the offer and asked for fifty million USD more. It was approved in no time.

Akhtar thought about Pakistan Global Bank. He had a card of a relationship manager there on his table. He never remembered the name. But he talked to a young man. He had to confirm the rates at his home bank first before looking out to transfer the bulk amount. Akhtar dialed the number from the card.

Zaidi guised as a banking advisor of Pakistan Global Bank picked up the phone. He cunningly managed to swap the original visiting card on Akhtar's table with this one. It was not the same mobile he normally used to attend calls.

"Hello! Good Afternoon Mr. Akhtar. How can I help you?"

"Hello Mr. Ahmed, I was just thinking of shifting the amount from the current account to term deposits for gaining some more interest from it. I talked with a few other banks but I want to check your rates before…"

"We have some extremely attractive rates. We have interest rates of 10.25."

"And, if I want to premature…"

"I am afraid, sir. We offer short term period deposits also. Premature results in penalty on interest accrued."

Akhtar already knew where he wanted to shift.

Next day, Akhtar Ahmed Shaikh was seating in the lush office room of United Bank of Pakistan. He was speaking to the General Manager, Corporate Banking of the company. After few talks of greetings, Akhtar came directly to the point.

"Look, I have a friend Murray Zaidi who is working in your bank, may be in some other department. He told me that the premature withdrawal in your bank is penalty free. I need to withdraw in partial or full at one or many instances as per the proceeding of work."

"Yeah. I know him. He is a brilliant guy. You can avail that facility. But it requires approval from higher authority. But, anyway, in this case it won't be an issue."

"One thing", Akhtar told, "Please don't spread the word that I am keeping bulk deposits in your bank in press now. Let the procedures be done and the cheque get credited"

"No issues, Akhtar."

Akhtar was satisfied. Zaidi told him not to make too much fuss in media before doing the shift. He obeyed his advice, he found it logical.
That day itself, the account was opened with a speed-gate facility in which the customer can get

the account number instantly and that very day itself the cheque book is provided to the customer.

Hector Fernandez guised as Murray Zaidi was waiting for a call at his residence, sipping freshly brewed hot coffee. He was looking tensed.

The call came after thirty minutes. He talked over the phone for next five minutes. And, when it was over, he turned to Soha, kissed her on her cheeks and told, "UBGC account is opened", the light kiss now turned to a passionate smooch as he held her sucking her tongue. The dripping passion and wild lust paused for a second just to say, "Tomorrow is your day, babe."

Soha on the next day went to another branch of United Bank of Pakistan in Kalat. The paperwork was ready. She was opening a current account of a private limited company whose name was Ugler Bailey Global Corporation.

The customer service executive on the other side was more than excited to hear this. "We just need a purpose letter from the authority and the documents of the partners"

The pretty receptionist took Soha to the branch head. She was provided a royal treatment. The manager convinced her to keep float balance in his branch and he will give any service at an instant. Soha also assured him on that. The turnover of Ugler Bailey, she told, was more than eight hundred million. She can if she wishes to maintain a considerable amount in her current account. A cheque of nearly hundred million was to be credited in some months. The manager was fluttered. *At last, he got a big fish.* Ugler Bailey was that very company which was deployed for construction purpose in Kalat. The whole fund of UBGC would basically be directed to this account only.

The account was opened.

Pakistani Global Bank (PGB) made queries regarding if their service was not adequate or what was the issue that made him shift to United Bank of Pakistan. Akhtar did not comment on those. He kept himself off from this. He called Zaidi and handed over the cheque of one hundred and fifty million dollars.

"Akhtar, can you just give me a printed advice to encash the cheque? Since, you will not fill up the deposit slip, just give me printed advice. Since, it is a big amount, you know, it is strict for Anti Money Laundering rules…"
"Well…"
Zaidi went over to his tab. "We have a format already. Let me fill it. And, you authorize or sign under."

It was all well. Akhtar read the whole advice. There was nothing suspicious. He signed it. What he didn't notice was – in the first sentence "I hereby advise you to credit the cheque number *012201* to my account name UBGC". What Akhtar didn't notice was a gap beside the name "UBGC".

Zaidi aka Hector placed the other account number after he signed in front of him only. And, post the word UBGC he put a slash and wrote Ugler Bailey Global Corporation.

Hector Fernandez was sitting in a café. Soha was sitting before him. His mind was racing. "My game is over. It is your turn now" he told smiling. "All the best."

Soha went to the branch. She deposited the cheque in the hand of the executive she met the day before and left the branch. In the afternoon, she got a call.

"Madam, I am branch manager of UBP. It is regarding your cheque you dropped today. There is a name mismatch. The cheque is bearing the name in short UBGC only."

"What! Ohh – *Dammit*! What will happen now? You cannot do it anyway? It is very urgent, you know. The amount is freaking hundred fifty million dollars."
"Can you provide us a written advice from your other part?"

"Let me check."

In half an hour, Soha entered the branch, straight to the room of branch head. She had the advice with her which Hector already prepared beforehand with Akhtar's signature and authorization below. "Please clear the cheque. I have the advice."

The cheque was cleared, and the amount is credited the very next day.

The trick was that it was the same United Bank of Pakistan where the money was credited. As he received mail intimation, Akhtar didn't minutely check the account number in detail.

While initially in the new account, they provided Akhtar's mail id, it was changed to a new one in the next day. With one hundred and fifty million dollars in account, the bank completed the service request in a few hours of time.

The next few days were the days of siphoning the fund. With internet banking at their disposal, Hector and Soha distributed the funds in two hundred different accounts. All of them were the members of the movement. Cash were withdrawn from the accounts readily. Being relatively smaller amounts, there was not much suspicion raised.

Soha, with her undying charm, convinced the branch manager to withdraw huge amount of cash for three consecutive days too.

And, after four days, the bank account was almost nearing zero. *They were done!*

Bakhtar Shaikh, the zonal head of United bank Of Pakistan was looking at the balances of various high net-worth accounts of his bank in his zone. Last week, he was on leave on occasion of his brother's marriage. In between also, he was intimated that his region has received one of the most important accounts of the country. It would not only boost his career but would boost the bank's performance also.

But as he was talking to the manager of that branch where UBGC account was opened in real, he was surprised to know that no money was ever credited in this account. Further probing revealed that a hefty one hundred and fifty dollars were credited to another account with name Ugler Bailey Global Corporation. Tracking the account transactions, he was trembling. A massacre is being done.

He immediately dialed a number. "Spread alert. Suspected laundering of one hundred and fifty million dollars!!"

There was a call from the intercom. Akhtar reluctantly picked up the phone. He was attending a call from his native place.
"Sir, police."
"What?"

In no time, he saw three big men standing in front of him. "We have a warrant to arrest you, Mr. Akhtar Ahmed Shaikh."

Everything seemed hazy. It seemed to be in some kind of déjà vu for him. Are they actors? Is it an April Fool Day?

He was handcuffed. He was put a black sack over his head. Outside the office was a huge crowd of reporters and common men. A fraud was caught. Akhtar was almost out of senses.

He faintly heard "The bastard stole hundred and fifty million dollars."

It seemed too dim for him to live. He could see the faults. *His faults. His trust. The friend who was reluctant talking business. The fake card of Pakistan Global Bank. The printed advice.*

But, they recognized Murray Zaidi and that he was on leave. Whatever, he thought and told himself, Akhtar Ahmed Shaikh was finished.

Murray Zaidi returned from his holidays. He was under viral fever. He even lost his mobile while returning home that day. It was about twenty days. Though he got well in five days back, his doctor insisted to rest at home for another five –six days. It felt him nice to be seated on his desk at office. He loved his job. He earned his name by sheer capability and hard work here. He suddenly saw two cops in front of him.

"Can you please come with us to the station? We don't want to create a scene here."

Hector and Soha were on a bike towards the place where Alam asked them to go for an escape plan for Hector. He was carrying a bag full of cash withdrawn from the bank. It started with pick-pocketing the mobile from Murray Zaidi and ended in a rush.

"But we scape-goated two honest men in the process."

"Zaidi will be released today only after routine interrogations. Akhtar will face the heat. But, police will leave him after few months of custody." he stopped, "Collateral damages are part of any work. You can't disregard the fact." He told as he rushed his bike through the dusty lanes of Kalat.

Chapter 7

As instructed by Ghalib for his escape, after a ride of almost thirty minutes, the bike screeched to stop in front of a warehouse. *It was time to part.* As Hector walked towards the entry door, he knew it was the last time that he could see Soha. And, he could see Soha smiling and waving at him.

"I can't go. It's time for me to act for my land. It's time for me to resist the oppression and the tyranny. If we escape for a bright life, our land will be doomed to darkness forever. Let me stay back." Soha told him when he once asked her to go with him. They were all trying to put up a resistance against the oppression. And, what Hector least could do was to help them raising funds. Help Ghalib. Be it by conning the system, he never minded that. For the system had conned them for ages. *For the system had conned him for life.*

As he heard the ignition of the bike, he turned back for a glimpse of Soha for the very last time. He couldn't see her eyes. It was covered in an oversized dark shade and a helmet with her hair falling straight on her shoulders. As he could see her ride away, he murmured, "Bella Ciao" to her and knocked on the door the warehouse.

A young guy opened the door. They seemed to be properly informed about him. As he entered, he was guided to the back of the warehouse, where there were a dozen containers, most of them filled and sealed, ready to be taken to the airport. There was one soft container half filled with wooden logs.

"Get in. Fast" the young guy was in a rush pointing to the one.

Hector took a deep breath, stepped into the container, and sat down. In a minute, a large piece of canvas dropped down on the opening. He could hear ropes being tied around to hold it up in place.

He could barely hear the voice telling him, "Don't move or make sound. I have made some holes. So you can breathe." He could hear his footsteps fading away.

The box was narrow and cramped, and a pile of wooden logs took up most of the space. As he started breathing short in claustrophobia, Ghalib's word almost were ringing on his ears. "*As soon as the police would learn of the robbery, they'll close the city tight. And, you'll have nowhere to hide. This is the only way to your country. There will be our men where this pallet will be opened. You'll be safe. Just don't forget to breathe in between.*" He winked, "*And, as you reach, say Hi to Kuldeep.*"

He must have dozed, for he was awakened with a start as the container was jerked into the air. Hector felt himself swinging in the air. He had to cling to the sides for support. There was a slam of a car door. The engine roared and he could hear the truck moving.

The whole plan was sketched by Ghalib on a very urgent note. Hector had to be poached out without a trace. Victor Patra of VP Cargos was a friend and sympathizer of Ghalib and their fight against state oppression. Based out of London, Patra had a strong connection with the politicians and who's who of Pakistan. Out of many businesses he ran, cargo was one of them. As Ghalib asked his help for a safe house to shelter Hector, Victor suggested this one. The operation had been personally instructed. As Hector moved along, he understood, he was not the first one en route this way.

The giant 747 *PIA* cargo plane was in process of being loaded. The nose had been raised, revealing the rows of tracks. The cargo containers were on a platform level with the opening, ready to slide across a bridge into the hold of the plane. There were almost forty pallets, few of them in the main deck and a few in the belly hold.

The loading was almost being completed. Aman Bhagat looked at his watch and cursed. The truck was late. All other consignments were loaded into its pallets and the canvas sides were fastened down with crisscross of ropes. As Bhagat was made aware of there would be an important consignment to be transported. *But hell!! Where's the truck?*

The loadmaster called, "What are we waiting for, Aman?"

"A minute," Bhagat answered. He hurried towards the entrance of the loading area. There was no sign of the truck.

"What's the issue?" he turned. A senior supervisor was coming towards him. "Get this cargo in the air. Fast!"

"Yes, sir. I was just waiting for..."

At that moment the truck from VP Cargo raced into the warehouse.

"Here's the last cargo." Bhagat announced.

He supervised the unloading of the container from the truck and sent it on the bridge leading to the plane.

Moments later the cargo was aboard and the nose of the plane was lowered into place. Bhagat watched as the jets were fired up and the giant plane started rolling towards the runway.

There was a fierce storm. The water level was increasing and he is drowning deep down into it. *I am drowning*, Hector thought. As he fought back to his senses from the nightmare, he recollected his conscious and found himself giddy. The plane hit a pocket of turbulence; Hector was thrown against the side of the box. He lay there. Dazed. *I must have air*. The air outside was cold. He was freezing. The constant jolting resulted in nausea. And, a second jolt in the turbulence and he was hit against the other side of the container. And, he lay there unconscious.

He was awakened by the slash of light hitting the inside of the truck as someone raised the canvas. The truck was in the warehouse of VP Cargo India in Delhi.

Dripping with perspiration and extreme headache, he watched, as he saw a tall shadow standing as the canvas is opening up. And through a haze vision, he could see Kuldeep Singh standing, "Welcome home. You all right?"

Hector's next two days were spent in the warehouse. As Kuldeep told him to wait for further instructions, Hector was made to work in the warehouse for the shipment of cargo.

As Kuldeep talked to him, he sensed, Faiz has matured to Hector. "Stay here till I instruct you." As Kuldeep was turning to leave, he just paused for a moment and turned to Hector, "Don't try to take law in your own hands in any case. Anything against the state is a serious offense."

"That's what I did there. Catalyze the fight against the oppression of the state." Hector's face was devoid of any expression. "Any oppression is a crime. And, I will fight against it." Hector came closer to Kuldeep. "And I don't mind which state I am fighting against."

Kudeep smiled calmly. "No state is criminal. It's the people running the state are responsible for the crimes. It's same there and here." He patted on Hector's shoulder. "Don't fight the state. Fight these people. The criminals."

Next few days Hector stayed at the warehouse. *Idle.* But that day, it was different. Their whole team was glued to the television from morning. It was the announcement of election results in Maharashtra. It was not about the victory of any party but the people were more interested in the fate of Shreya Basu. *The new sensation of Indian politics.* As he saw various glimpses of Shreya in the following news capsules throughout the day, he knew what led her to become such a sensation. India never saw such a suave, highly educated and beautiful politician in ages. Each of her interviews proved her knowledge. And, her appealing face and a toned body was enough to make her a dream lady for many. And, it was the first time that Indians were voting someone out of sheer love and appreciation.

The whole episode of announcement of results was a bore. Shreya Basu went on to win majority of seats. But the twist came towards the end when it was evident that Shreya's party would be single largest party of the state. The other two parties made a coalition to appeal to the governor of the state to form government. The drama went on for few hours till the time governor decided to give them fifteen days of time to prove their majority through voting in Mantralaya. *One who wins there forms government.* The coalition parties were already on a celebrating mode. Many of the MLAs were giving bites on television. And, suddenly, he came across Afzal Shaikh on television. He was representing the area Hector and their family used to live once. He won and being an influential person, he was a sure shot to be in the cabinet of the chief minister.

And, watching his face and voice, Hector was living his past. He was hearing his mother's voice calling him. He could feel his brother's breathe on his shoulder calming him down. *And, then that day when he was asked to identify his body lying dead on the tracks on railway. Separated from his head. And, then the row of gloomy nightmare-like life...*

They can't win. He thought. *In a democracy where people's say gives power, they required to be ripped off it. It's not death but the loss of power is what will ground them first.*

While media was busy speculating the cabinet ministers of the coalition government, Hector was in his room. *Silent.*

Chapter 8

Monsoons in Mumbai are an experience in itself. With constant downpour round the clock – the city fights hard to keep itself afloat amidst the logging water. And, if the heavy rain doubles up with a high-tide, it becomes a case of serious concern. But the city never stops. It's this undying spirit of survival that keeps the city running.

Hector reached his old place of Mumbai. He was soaked in the nostalgia of his past days as he broke open the locked door to his small room. He could still see the paintings he made on their walls with pastel color pencils during his childhood. He could still hear his brother Junaid's voice calling him. And, his mother. As he entered their kitchen, he could still smell the aroma of his mother's chicken curry or those *parathas* on a Sunday morning. The Sunday afternoons – when he used to savor rice and mutton curry and then a long nap. The bed still lay there. *Secluded. Bereaved.* But it was not supposed to be like this. It was due to a dirty game that they were succumbed to this situation which ruined his family.

It was late evening and it was pouring heavily. *July months in Mumbai are like that only.* The whole colony was in a slumber. Afzal Shaikh was in his room. He had his dinner a bit early today. He was waiting for his wife to come in. The rains had restricted his pleasure plays for two consecutive days. One thing that he couldn't control was his urge to mate. Normally he would prefer to sleep before his wife's arrival to room, but he was wide awake today. Salma was almost twelve years younger to Afzal. When they were married, Afzal was a known name in Mumbai politics. *He was a powerful man.* And, Salma's family was a friend to Afzal's. With a pinkish-white complexion and a dimpled-cute face and full lips, Salma was a one-glance choice for Afzal. But the liking was short-lived. Impregnating her in the first few months itself, Afzal moved on to his other girls. And, Salma, slowly being projected as a beautiful housewife, remained aside as a prized possession of a powerful man. But Afzal never enjoyed mating with her. He found her too passive to his wildness. But with last two days being dry, he was up for banging. And, as soon as she entered, Salma found herself arrested in his arms. Tight. In a whisk, she was naked wriggling under his huge body. Her delicate body was roughed up by him. He pounced on her nubile breasts like a hungry lion. And, a short foreplay was followed by his huge manhood entering her. *Hard.* His strokes inside were mastered to arouse even the coldest of the bodies. And, the initial mellow strokes slowly gained momentum into rapid, wild and hard throbs. After almost a stretch of forty minutes and Salma came twice, she sensed a presence of a third party in their room. But she couldn't see anybody. Though she tried to tell Afzal, he was behind her pumping vigorously from the back, holding her hair tight and moaning as he was about to come. Salma could hear the movement of the person inside and in a while she could see a lean, tall man calmly taking his seat in the chair in front of her. And, in that moment, she felt the hot gushing deep down inside her and Afzal fell on her back panting.

Hector sat there. As Afzal released and opened his tired eyes, he was startled by his presence. He raised his voice. "How dare you bastard?" Salma went on to get her clothes.

Hector smiled at him. "You should be happy that I waited for your pleasure to end else I would have shot your head with your dick still inside her." He poised his gun. He crossed his legs and leaned back on his chair yawning calmly. "But I have time today. And, you have a lot to tell."

"What do you want?"

"Tell me what led to my brother's murder?... Who killed him?"

As Hector was walking along the empty shores of the Marine Drive with high-tide lashing on the sides, he was reeling in his mind the episode as Afzal confessed to him. *The problem was deep-rooted in the system,* he thought, *it was not Afzal or for that matter the racket involved in this scam. The problem lay in us too. We vote them knowing them to be the culprits. We bowed down before them as they ask money to get what is righteously ours. We flock to listen to them delivering speeches of lies and clap and hoot despite knowing none of them would ever be realized anyway. Why do we do that? Is it for a favor that we expect from them? Why Junaid did not took them to law? Was it because he didn't have money? Else would he have also succumbed to their offer?* He has jolted back to senses by a policeman. "Move from here. It's high tide. It's not safe now. Go home and sleep." Had the policeman known he lost his home.

The Exam scam was a lingering issue that was bothering the incumbent government for long. As Afzal confessed it was operated from the senior leaders. They were just the pawns kept in front. The leaders like Manoj Pawar – the current Chief Minister would also get a part of the money involved in the scam. And, those who dared to dissent – the order was to finish them off. Junaid was also asked to kill. And, Afzal obeyed that. He was a potential threat. So, was Hector himself or his family and also, journalist Anjum Gupta. As he continued speaking, Hector realized that it was not just a single incident. There were dozens of Afzals operating in the same way and dozens of Junaids getting killed and dozens of families getting ruined. Without even pressurizing much, he found out several video calls, recorded phone calls from registered numbers from various members of the party. He also got to know the procedure how they used to launder this money and infuse this into the system to make it a legitimate fund. And, just when Hector understood, he had enough for the day, he decided to leave. As he went near the door keeping behind a sobbing Afzal Shaikh, he stopped and looked back. "Why don't you dress up and come with me?... It's raining lovely outside."

It was in the next morning that a mutilated body of Afzal Shaikh was found on the track of Mumbai Western Railways. The killing and the condition of the body was much similar to the case of Junaid Ahmed whose body was found almost at the same place only a few months back. Like Junaid Ahmed, Afzal Shaikh's head was also separated from the body and was found within the bushes near the railway track. As police was considering the possibility of a serial killer operating in this area, they tightened the security to protect the citizens from further such incidents.

As he was asked by the policeman to go, Hector was aimlessly wandering along the empty streets in the wee hours of the day; he was keeping a watch on the time. For he knew he had some place to go. And, its time he should reach there.

Chapter 9

Bhavna Mirza was lucky. On her first assignment, she would be covering the most anticipated political incident of the country. It was a democratic battle to be fought on the floor of the Vidhan Bhavan of Mumbai to decide who would form the government. *The whole country would be following this.*

Bhavna Mirza was a slender, curly-haired girl of twenty-four with a pale skin, an intelligent, mobile face, and dark-brown thoughtful eyes. It was a face that was more attractive than beautiful. A face that reflected pride. Courage. Sensitivity. And, it's hard to forget once seen.

Her day started in a disastrous way. The induction program at the AND News had been scheduled for nine A.M. sharp. Bhavna had carefully arranged her dress the night before and also had set alarm at six. As she stayed in Versova, she would have enough time to reach Bandra Kurla Complex, the HQ of AND where the induction was scheduled.

But the alarm failed somehow to go off. Bhavna was awakened at eight and panicked. She had rushed to shower but the Municipality water supply was not there. She had slammed the door of her apartment only to remember that she had left her keys inside. She planned to take a pool cab but now at the peak price she had to take a cab she could hardly afford. And, on her entire way to office, the cab driver kept her telling why they require Shreya Basu as their Chief Minister.

When Bhavna finally arrived, she was fifteen minutes late.

There were twenty new interns gathered in the hall, all of them newly out of Business Schools, young and eager and super excited to be working for one of the most prestigious and popular news channels of the country.

The office was quite impressive, paneled and decorated in good taste. Many people, dressed in impeccable formals, were rushing. The induction hall was at the other corner of the floor. There was a large conference table with chairs around it and at the corner there was a comfortable leather chair. On the walls there were framed pictures of Joseph Pulitzer, Bob Woodward and William Hearst.

When Bhavna hurried into the hall, full of apologies, Naresh Rajput, the owner of AND Broadcast Pvt Ltd was in the middle of a speech. He stopped, turned his attention on Bhavna and said, "What the hell do you think this is – kitty party?"

"I'm sorry, I -"

"I just give a damn whether you are sorry. Come in and you don't ever be late again!"

The nineteen others in the hall were carefully hiding their sympathy. Rajput turned to the group and snapped. "We are the news channel that has twice the viewership of all other channels combined. Our advertisement slots are of high demand. A ten second advertisement slot during the break of my *Prime Time Debate* program exceeds the slot rate during an India-Pakistan One-day match." As he walked behind the chair. "Politicians, actors and all other who's who are all after us for a small sneak in any of our news capsule." He looked audaciously proud. "We are powerful. And, you should be grateful to your destiny that you've got an opportunity to work with the team who creates news that others follow. You all have to be on your toes always brimming with energy and your intellect should overpower all others. Don't fear anything for you being an AND representative are always in a position to control." Rajput nodded to his assistant. "Do the requisite formalities."

As Rajput was walking around the floor, he was followed by the group of twenty new interns. With wide eyes, they were ogling their future desks and their senior colleagues. They were all hit by the wave of energy on the floor. As he entered his lavish room at the other corner of the floor, he lit a short, stubby cigar. "We have a huge event to be covered tomorrow. Can any of you tell what it is?"

Bhavna's hand was first one up. "Floor Test at Vidhan Bhavan."

Rajput looked at his assistant. "Why don't I use three of them to run errands for me tomorrow?"

As they left the room, three of them including Bhavna were given identity cards of AND News. *So, I will be a part of that historic moment of Indian democracy tomorrow*, she thought.

As she got back home that day, she sat in front of a photo of her father and revive the incidents on first day in office. *He would listen.* She was very close her father. Bhavna's father was attorney, mostly for the stumbling companies of the area. Her childhood memories of growing up were filled with joy. It was a story-book place for a child, full of spectacular natural beauty. There were hills all around. The mystic Tibetan monasteries were symbolic of the peace of mind. She used to visit the Bhagsu waterfall with her father. She learnt gymnastic and was a voracious trekker in the hills. She had sheer courage. She had un-put-down-able fitness. And, that added up extra spice to her persona.

Her father always had time for her, while her mother always remained mysteriously busy. She was seldom at home. Bhavna adored her father. Azan Mirza was a man of principles. He was tall and fair with sharp features and deep brown eyes. He was a compassionate man. And, he also had a deep-rooted sense of justice. Money never was able to lure him. Azan's love was for people. He felt a deep sense of gratification by helping people and bringing on justice. He would sit and talk to Bhavna about the cases he was dealing.

After school Bhavna would hurry over to the court to watch her father work. If the court was not in session she would watch her father discussing cases. When Bhavna was sixteen, she started working for her father in her summer and winter holidays. At the age of eighteen, when other girls were dating boys, she was mostly absorbed in lawsuits and wills. Though her father wanted her to be in law, Bhavna dreamt of being in media. And, Azan was happy. *Her little girl had made a choice.*

On her nineteenth birthday, her mother died in a car-crash while coming back from Dharamshala. Her father was highly aggrieved and started drinking heavily. Soon, Azan Mirza started on a case that questioned the business functioning of a government owned firm and the internal corruption that was accused of tampering public money. He was fighting for a person who claimed it through RTI Act. Though all documents were in place, the state High Court rubbished the accusation. Aggrieved by the rejection, Azan Mirza moved to the Supreme Court. For the first time in his life, he was in media. Reports started showering about him. Bhavna was in her college. She used to keep her eyes on television channels always keeping a tab on all adjectives used on her father. She collected all newspapers featuring news with the name of her father.

But soon, the hell broke loose. He was approached by the opponent parties. But, Azan Mirza was a strict man. He was never interested to get his hands dirty and biased. He rejected all approaches.

And, slowly, he was accused of communal favors for the client he was serving was of his religion. *He was trapped.* Azan Mirza knew he lost the game. The powerhouse media were all accusing him. *Without proof.* The prime time television debates already declared him an anti-national.

But Azan Mirza was not a man to bow down. He pursued his case. The next dates of appeal delayed, postponed and forgotten. He was accused of titillating communal provocation. He was arrested. He was interrogated and was out on a bail.

He got back to McLeod Ganj. His own town looked unfamiliar with suspicious eyes of people all around. It took three long years for his heart to stop beating, but he was very dead from the moment he was accused. The whole town was either suspicious or sympathetic, and, that of course made it worse, since Azan Mirza was a man of pride and honor.

Bhavna was in her last year of degree. She wanted to stay back home with her father. But Azan never agreed, "You first go and get that degree."

When she graduated, she was on for a higher degree. And, on her holiday to her town she was sitting by her ailing drunken father. He told her, "You will be working in media. You should know", he coughed rough. Then controlling himself, he continued, "They have abolished the middle path. Either you are pro or against. You don't have a right to dislike either. Strange" he coughed and cleared his voice. "But, should a media be biased? Has it got to be red or green?" He laughed sarcastically and then told. "The media is ought to be a *protanopic* in that case."

He died when Bhavna was in her first year of her masters. The town remembered, and there were almost two hundred people at the funeral of Azan. Bhavna was numb. It was like losing the heart. She had lost more than a father. She had lost a teacher and a mentor at the same time.

After the funeral she returned to Delhi to complete her masters in Mass Communication and she passed out in flying colors. She bagged a job from the campus recruitment drive at the famous AND News Corp as an intern.

Bhavna did her homework well. She researched all night about the current condition of both the parties and that the coalition is two seats ahead of Shreya Basu's Reds. With even an unfortunate death of Afzal Shaikh, where there would be re-election, the coalition was a seat ahead. It would be a smooth victory for them. Even Naresh Rajput who was himself there for coverage expected that Shreya Basu would retract from the floor test. In one of the Facebook Live that they did out of the Vidhan Bhavan, Rajput also told that it was the only way out for her to save her reputation and also retain public love for walking over was better than fighting for an inevitable loss. But till then, she didn't give any information for her setback. Moreover, they could see Red MPs also coming slowly. They were mostly avoiding media and looking clueless. Bhavna was acutely following everything she got to see.

She watched outside as Shreya Basu came to Vidhan Bhavan. With a large number of her supporters and media going crazy on her arrival, Bhavna found her quite impeccable in appearance and attitude. *There's something about her,* she thought, *or maybe she's the one whom we wanted to see for long.*

Shreya Basu reached Vidhan Bhavan in her dark grey Volvo XC90. With a dark blue saree and oversized shades, she was looking as elegant and attractive as a film heroine would die to look like. As she stepped down from her car waving hand to people standing to support her, the media went crazy to get a small bite from her. Like she would never shy away from the media, she steadily approached them with a calm smile and just told, "Please keep calm. We are the single largest party of the state and we'll form government."

With an inevitable loss on cards, such confidence startled everyone. *How she can be so confident even at this point of time when her time to defeat can be counted in minutes,* Bhavna thought as she saw her enter and take seat in the front row with Malik following her.

She saw Naresh Rajput rose to his feet. He was talking to the coalition leaders surrounding her. His counterparts were setting up their camera and doing Facebook Live or Instagram Live with several opposition leaders. The Red leaders were mostly avoiding getting online or giving bites.

Manoj Pawar and Mahesh Shinde looked relaxed and giving bites to several media houses. The coalition was in a mood to chill. As Rajput started off with a Facebook Live with Mahesh Shinde almost declaring him as the Chief Minister, Bhavna watched a tall, lean man saying something to Rajput and hurried over towards her. He was carrying a mobile phone in his him. "Miss Mirza?"

Bhavna looked up in surprise. "Yes."

"Mr. Rajput wants you to give this to Manoj sir, there." He handed over a mobile phone with the screen paused while running a video. "This is something important that he would know before the floor test starts. It's regarding a speech that is needed to be given."

As she got the mobile phone and looked at Rajput, she felt well. *He remembered my name,* she thought, *it's a good omen.*

"Better get moving. And tell him he should think along these lines before he speaks next. There's hardly any time left for the test."

"Yes sir." Bhavna rose to her feet.

As she approached Manoj Pawar, he was working on his own mobile. "Mr. Rajput told to watch this and think along the lines before your speech."

Manoj Blinked and started the video.

Chapter 10

With every minute passing by, the pressure was building on the Reds. Malik was getting restless in his room with calls coming from media and party members every second minute. They all were interested in what the great mind of Adbul Rashid Malik was thinking.

Srinivas was in his bed. He was too old and weak to discuss the strategy and Malik didn't want to bother him too. *That person was never after power*, Malik thought, *even now he tells us how important it is to oppose the policies correctly and keep the incumbent government on toes.* But the dynamics of politics is on a different landscape now. It's very important to display power and position to get noted.

He would dial Shreya's number now and then and both after a few updates would share silences. There were questions that couldn't be answered. It was unacceptable that with such an unprecedented love and support from people, they failed. It was a strategic miss. Naresh Rajput, *that bastard,* played games with them. Last night one of his core team members even had a conversation over the phone with both Malik and Shreya in the conference. For forming government next day, he demanded free operation of his business teams in the state. And, he wouldn't allow any interference. The police and state would keep their hands off. And, if any allegation ever arises, the state would provide complete support. He, to some extent, even confessed their involvement in the State Exam scam along with the incumbent government people.

The conditions were too much to maintain. But the stakes were high too. If the Reds would lose this one, all the hype surrounding the image of Shreya Basu that was built up in last few months would fade. It would be impossible for them to survive. The whole bait would go doldrums. Rajput asked them to let him know their decision by the first hour of the next day.

Malik, being trapped in a dilemma like never before, was lighting fags after fags and ignoring all phone calls. He was even receiving text messages from his MLAs stating if it was required to be present in the Vidhan Bhavan or they were pulling out of the contest. He didn't know what to do. But he couldn't even succumb to the conditions set by Rajput.

She couldn't remember when the last time she was broken like this. *May be she was like this after hearing the news of his father's demise.* But this pressure was different. It was more than losing something. It was a loss that was not only concerning her. There were lakhs of people who voted for her. They all showered support to her. Her loss signified the loss of all these people who believed in her. Malik. The Reds. With a heavy heart and a wary mood, she went to shower. With a glass of red wine in her hand, she stepped into the warm tub of water, slowly sinking down into it feeling the luxury of the water lapping over her body. She had not realized how mentally exhausted she was. She decided to have a good dinner to cheer her up. But before that she had to do one important thing. She would call Malik once and tell him the decision of withdrawal from the floor test. This was the only option left. And, Malik had left the final decision on her. As soon as she would inform him, he assured her that he would arrange for a press conference to declare the same.

I was wrong. Politics is not for me. I would rather get back to London and settle myself with a job. This is not for me…

Her thought was interrupted by the ringing of the doorbell. *Room Service. But at this hour?*

Reluctantly, she dragged herself from the warm tub. She slipped on a silk robe and went to the door. She decided to send him back. She needed seclusion. But as soon as she opened the door a man in the dress of a room service barged in, "Sorry. I didn't intend to. But there is no way too. So, …" he looked at her appreciably, "Though you're looking absolutely great, I would keep that for another day."

Shreya whipped back, "Who the hell are you?" she reached out her phone to dial 100.

"I am Hector Fernandez. Defense Intelligence."

"But this is not the way to intrude into a civilian's house."

"I know. But I don't have time and intent to follow any procedure. We needed to talk and that's something important. And, that's required to be done, right now."

There was something in his voice. May be it was the pain that touched her. She calmed down. "Ok. Tell me. What is it?"

"If you can just change into something that wouldn't distract me, unlike your current attire, that would help me concentrate better ..." Shreya smiled and went to the other room to slip into a long sleeping gown with a housecoat over it. "Hope this helps." She told as she approached. It was only a few minutes, but she had started feeling comfortable with the stranger in her room.

"Don't walk out tomorrow. Call and confirm that you'd require every single MLAs from your party to be present there. You're going to win."

As she was giving him a *what-the-heck* kind of a look, he snapped, "I have something to show you." He took out a mobile phone and showed him a few videos. Manoj Pawar was seen taking update on the Maharashtra State Commission Examinees list and how many of them were called and what was the expected amount. On another video, Satish Nayak, the MLA from Jalgaon was making a video call to Afzal Shaikh and explaining the way to siphon these funds outside. Several times some big names were taken like Mahesh Shinde and other MLAs. Hector also showed her bank documents and even foreign bank details of accounts where the money was siphoned and again infused and utilized in various political campaigns and for personal gains of many politicians. It would require a few hours of interrogation to catch the whole racket. There were evidences of thousands of crores being siphoned out and money remitted inwards to Naresh Rajput's shell companies' account and then again got distributed.

Smile appeared in Shreya's face. Her heart was beating hard and fast. The excitement was too much to hold.

Hector was leaning back on the sofa. "Just call and confirm. See you tomorrow at the battleground."

"But why are you helping me to win?"

Hector stopped moment while walking out. "It's not about you winning." He turned back with his face firm and eyes intense. "It's about them losing and me winning."

Shreya did not believe what was happening. She even once pinched herself to realize that she was not dreaming. And, with her being convinced that it happened in real, she called Malik. "We're going tomorrow to Vidhan Bhavan. Please ask everybody of our team to be present there. We're going to win."

Malik was startled. "Are you in senses?"

"Like never before." She hung. *There was something in the person's words that filled her with confidence. Or is it her unflinching desire to chair the state that is hindering her all logical senses.* She didn't have any answer. *Or she didn't want to answer.*

Next, she dialed the number of Naresh Rajput. "Hi Ms. Chief Minister", the sarcasm was evident. "Tell me what have you decided."

"I am not accepting your conditions and also not moving out of the contest, Rajput."

"Are you out of mind, Ms Chief Minister or your Jack Daniels is having too much an effect?"

"Check yourself, Rajput. Your sarcasm if comes true, you'd not even get a day to save your ass."

"In your dreams, lady."

Chapter 11

Bhavna was making her way inside the Vidhan Bhavan among the rows. There were many broadcasters setting up their camera. There were many reporters having chats with the politicians. Situated in the famous Nariman Point area and just across the sea, the Vidhan Bhavan is an exquisite locale. Two hundred and eighty-eight members of Legislative Assembly were selected from the single seat constituencies. The budget session of the state and the monsoon session were convened here while the winter session used to be convened in Nagpur. Being the floor with one of the highest number of Legislative Assembly members of the country, the Bhavan was of utmost political importance. And, she braced herself to be a part of this in her initial days itself. She was brought to senses by the hum on the other end of the hall. Walking along, she went far from the place where Manoj Pawar was sitting. She could see a gathering of few members. And, the crowd was moving to the direction of the corridor with Manoj Pawar seeming to be leaving the house. She hurried to the corridor. It was bedlam. People were racing around frantically. Guards armed with guns had taken up positions at the exit door. Reporters who had been making their stories live were rushing to the corridors and calling their counterparts outside. Far down she could see Naresh Rajput frantically issuing orders to his reporters. His face drained out of colors.

My God, he's going to have a heart attack, Bhavna thought.

She pushed her way through the crowd and moved towards him, thinking perhaps she could be of some help. As she approached, one of the deputies who had been guarding Manoj Pawar looked up and saw Bhavna. He raised an arm and pointed to her and in less than a few seconds Bhavna Mirza found herself being grabbed and taken along. She could see in the far front row, Shreya Basu was calmly working on her mobile without even looking behind anytime as if nothing was happening.

She was made to sit on one of the chairs and she could find the frowning faces of hundreds of people around her.

Naresh Rajput was leaning so close to her that Bhavna could see the vein in his temple. "Who paid you to give that mobile to Manoj?"

"Paid me? Nobody paid me!" his voice started quavering with indignation.

Mahesh Shinde shot her with, "Nobody paid you? You just walked up and gave this mobile?"

Bhavna stared at the mobile phone in his hand. Horrified. "One of your men – gave me -"

"Which one of my men - ?"

"I – I don't know."

"You don't know who it was, but you know it was one of my men." His voice rang with disbelief.

It's all a nightmare. I would wake up anytime and it will be six o' clock in the morning.

"How Much?"

His voice was overruled by a humming voice. And, people came around for her rescue from the situation. The speaker of the Assembly Mr. Anil Tambe was asking for all to rest. The floor test was going to begin.

Mahesh Shinde rose to his feet and went to the speaker. He would put forward the request of coalition to form government given the fact that with Afzal Shaikh's death and Manoj Pawar walking out, the number of seats of the coalition was equal to that of the Reds.

Naresh Rajput knew it was a lost battle. Shreya Basu won the bait being the single largest party. With a last-minute twist, she had made sure that not only Manoj Pawar, but many including him behind the bars for a long time to come. Even if they re-contest Afzal Shaikh's area, it would be a cake walk for Shreya.

The next few minutes went dizzy for Bhavna. So was the case for Naresh Rajput and the other party members with drops of perspiration around their face. Not only that Shreya in some minutes would be on the dais taking the oath in as the Chief Minister of the state but they would be put to rest in days to come. And, Naresh Rajput knew one thing well. With Malik and Shreya together, he would be hit the hardest of them all.

A Few Hours Back

Hector Fernandez had lots of things to do. It would have to be done with utmost care. He got a video call from Manoj Pawar directly asking Afzal to demand two lakh rupees minimum for a single seat of the State Commission Exam. The tactics was simple. He just had to hand it over to him. Sending it beforehand was a risk. It may get ignored or there would be time to create a defense against it. It had to be sudden to get him strangled and eventually exit. With an equal number of seat and Reds being the single largest party, the incumbent party and their alliance would be thrown out of power.

The most important thing was to enter the *Bhavan* and then handing it over to Manoj. It would be tough given the fact that he would always be surrounded by people around. And, he would not suddenly accept something from a stranger. He had to get a media person involved. But that would be impossible at this late hour, particularly with such a short time at hand. But he had to think it out.

Vidhan Bhavan had its own canteen. The tender of the same used to be given to several private bodies that used to serve them during the sessions. This floor test being a sudden incident, they had to select someone from their existing tender holder to do the needful. While going through many recorded phone calls and documents, Hector went across a call where Manoj Pawar asked Afzal to arrange for the same. As he searched more, he found that he gave it to a company called Pink Foods and Hospitality Pvt Ltd. That morning he went to Pink Foods company office. It was a small office in the Grant Road area. Meeting their chief, Mr. Azhar Shaikh, Hector put forth a list.

"Manoj Pawar sent me on behalf of Afzal sir as you must be knowing about his sad demise."

"These people had such recommendations. As you must know some of our ministers had pressure or sugar. So, this had to be taken into consideration while giving them food or tea for that matter."

"But my team already left for Vidhan Bhavan." Azhar looked puzzled.

"No issues. Just let them know." He handed over the file with names against each favorite listed there." As you know they will be swearing-in-ceremony today, so he wouldn't want anybody to be kept unsatisfied as far as refreshments are concerned."

Azhar Shaikh was a young man who had recently taken over Pink Foods' ownership after his father's health had not gone well. And, this was the first time that he was handling something of importance other than a few marriage ceremonies that he had served and he didn't want things to go wrong in any case.

"I can help you. If you can tell me whom to contact I can visit him there and instruct him accordingly so that no mess ups happen."

Azhar looked as he just got his heart beating once again. *Relieved*. He held his hand. "Thank you."

"But I would require your ID once to get through."

"Sure."

As he got out of that office, Hector was relieved that now he at least had an entry to the spot.

The entry process was seamless. He had the ID of the hospitality company and after a few checks, he entered. The area was completely vacant with only hospitality people working in the canteen area. As he entered, he was greeted by their supervisor, Mr. Vikas Mehta. "Azhar sir told you'd be coming." Graduated from a premier Hotel management school, Vikas was a polished manager. He had previously supervised hundreds of events involving the international summits in India and abroad. As Hector sat with him and started talking on the list, he heard people entering into the Bhavan. As he completely delivered the fictitious list to him, Hector rose to his feet and asked for his leave.

As he went out of the canteen, Hector kept his eyes on Naresh Rajput and a dozen people following him. Some of them were carrying various cameras and instruments for live shows. A few of them seemed to be too young to be present here. Hector wondered. Following their actions for a few minutes, he got to understand these three young people were interns brought here to run errands for the senior journalists.

Scanning each of their activities thoroughly, Hector was looking for the one best suited for handing over the mobile phone to Manoj Pawar. *It can't go wrong,* he thought.

Then his eyes fell on the slim, fair and attractive girl. *She is looking a bit overwhelmed. She is looking to be over conscious about herself. Insecured. These people are easy to convince! She is looking around the building. She is following the people here intensely. She is overwhelmed to be present here. Oh yes, she is new here! She is following Naresh Rajput like her idol. She will be pleased to do anything for him. May be, it is her first day out. But she is left with no work… she is the one.*

He looked at her ID, Bhavna Mirza.

As he made his way into the gathering around Naresh Rajput, she saw her eyes on him too. Naresh was too busy to look at him. He just acted as if he was telling something to Naresh and made his out to her in hurried steps. He was carrying the mobile phone with him. "Miss Mirza?"

"Yes." He saw her young bright eyes looking at him surprised.

"Mr. Rajput wants you to give this to Manoj sir, there." He handed over the mobile phone with the screen paused while running the video. "This is something important that he would know before the floor test starts. It's regarding a speech that is needed to be given." He could clearly see her eyes brimming with happiness. *Rajput remembering a new entrant is a big deal,* he thought.

To bring her to senses to her utopic moment, he snapped. "Better get moving. And tell him he should think along these lines before he speaks next. There's hardly any time left for the test."

"Yes sir."

He saw her approaching Manoj Pawar and handing over the mobile phone. *Done!* He made his way out towards the exit gate. On his way out, he stared once at Shreya Basu sitting on the front row working on her mobile. Her silky straight hair falling on her saree and those impeccable attractive eyes could arouse one even at the highest tensed moments.

The Governor had taken decision. He asked Shreya Basu to take oath in the ceremony as the Chief Minister of the state. The oath taking ceremony took place the very next day. Mahesh Shinde and Manoj Pawar didn't challenge the decision. They were more worried about their own fate and tried to contact Malik and Shreya for a deal. But they couldn't get in touch with either.

For Hector Fernandez had kept two conditions forth to her. One that the culprits of the scams should be arrested the very next day of her becoming the Chief Minister and the second one he told was personal but needed to be convened before the first one itself.

Chapter 12

Shreya Basu stood naked, staring out of the large picture window of her suite on the top floor of the hotel she was staying overlooking the magnificent Arabian Sea. It was a beautiful, crisp day.

"Mumbai is really mesmerizing." She whispered in his ears.

Hector Fernandez looked at her body. "So are you." And, in moments, his hands were on her breasts caressing them. "Let's get back to bed."

His touch made Shreya shiver. He demanded things that no man had even dared asking her. He did things that had never been done to her.

Shreya had never known anyone like Hector Fernandez. He was years younger to her. But his maturity was way ahead of his age. He was insatiable. His body was lean, hard and athletic. And, when on bed, it naturally would become a part of Shreya's body carrying her along in a wave of pounding excitement that went for infinity till she screamed aloud with wild joy. And, then again it started with an ecstatic charm of reaching the undefined space of bodily pleasure till it was almost too much to bear for both of them. Hector almost possessed her during the lovemaking. The frantic changes in him from a gentle kisser in mouth to a cruel, demanding and pounding bull all in a single session made her crazy. He would withdraw from her, teasing her to demand more, pleading. "Please take me." and, his hard organ would start pounding her once again. This time more vigorously than ever… till she screamed with pleasure. Hector stayed with her for a few hours.

Shreya lay on her bed. She wasn't sure what the attraction was all about. *Gratitude, yes.* But that was the small part of it. Was it the necessity of her to be subdued after the over-tensed and near-losing situation? May be.

She had no answer.

But one thing, she was sure about. And, as he left, she knew that she was never going to meet him again. *Or anyone like him.*

Bhavna Mirza was still trying to make sense what happened to her.

It was a nightmare. I would wake up anytime. She was terminated from AND. And, she was termed as a corrupted individual by them.

"We will take care of you." Many SMSs came in this line. She confined herself inside the four walls of her room. She didn't eat anything. She had nowhere to go. She had no money to pay rent. She was sure that she wouldn't be allowed in any news agency given her current reputation. Though Shreya Basu was the news for last two days for her nail-biting win, she was in the news too with her face flashing as the catalyst to the victory. But she didn't know Shreya Basu or anyway connected to her. She was trapped in a net she could hardly find a way out.

She was brought to senses by an alien sound in her room. It was the bell ringing. But it was the first time she was hearing this after a week of shifting here. As she half opened the door to see who was on the other side, her blood started boiling. It was the same face who handed her the mobile that day. Hector Fernandez. He pushed open the door to enter. Bhavna was trembling in excitement. Hector was calmly moving around the room till he made himself comfortable on a chair placed beside the bed and waived her to sit on the bed. And, she burst into tears and started rambling. All that Hector could make out of her rambling was. "Why?"

"I wouldn't take much of your time. Just check these and there are ample online sites where you can post this. Anyway, AND will perish in a few days. You can create your own by yourself. Good Luck."

Bhavna saw the man out of the room in seconds. There were piles of documents and a hard disc kept on the bed.

Shreya Basu tapped her desk impatiently with a MontBlanc fountain pen. The Police Commissioner she had a meeting with regarding the handling of increasing crowds for the civil uprising, was late for their 12 o'clock meeting. And, if there were one thing that Shreya hated, it was being late.

The civil uprising was due to Government's inaction on the State Exam Commission row. With one day on this chair, she knew how to crack down this.

A girl has leaked all the videos one by one on her YouTube channel exposing the who's who of the Maharashtra politics arena. The people went crazy on these videos and demanded immediate action and the arrests to be done. But she needed a bit of time. The uproar needed to be severe. The wrath of people should be on highest point. Naresh Rajput should understand that when the Sun shines down, even the worst predictions come true.

"Madam? Police Commissioner has arrived."

Shreya's permanent private secretary, Robert D'costa, broke her reverie. Immaculate as ever in a shining white shirt and a neat black trouser with his hair smoothed flat against his scalp, Robert smelled faintly of his Old Spice after shave.

Shreya looked at her watch. "What about the time? My day just got squeezed."

"I know madam. This shouldn't take too long".

Epilogue

The next seven days were the biggest track down by Mumbai Police in ages. The whole Police department along with Central Intelligence Department and State Intelligence Department worked hand in hand to arrest the worst possible racket that was selling government jobs resulting in missed opportunities for the deserving youths.

First time, the country saw the Prime Minister openly promising all central body assistances to get the guilty punished despite them being from the same party he belonged. Mahesh Shinde and Manoj Pawar were pulled out of their places and thrown into jail in days. Naresh Rajput was also arrested from the AND news Head Quarter at Bandra Kurla Complex in Mumbai. They were all denied bail and even lawyers were wary of fighting their cases with so much evidences already going viral on air. And, added to that there were immense pressure from civil society with their protest marches getting momentum every day and also the media started back-firing them. Though Rajput made efforts to portray this incident as a political game using his own media houses, the situation was too much out-of-hand for him to make people believe in his conspiracy theory.

The whole state was hailing the strong steps of Shreya Basu to arrest them.

"You know, what Albert Einstein once said? He said that, the world will not be destroyed by those who do evil, but by those who watch them without doing anything…" Shreya Basu told while giving interview to a news channel. And, she did make no mistake in giving her first ever interview as a Chief Minister to the girl who dared to upload the videos with voiceover explaining the offences in detail. It was Bhavna Mirza.

The Prime Minister of India visited the state and had a long meeting with Shreya Basu on various policies and issues pertaining to the state. After the meeting they held a press conference stating that central government would provide full support and work hand in hand with state government for the development.

Bhavna Mirza was an overnight sensation. Post her action in Vidhan Bhavan, her release of videos with voice over explaining the actions on her own YouTube channel exposed the hypocrisy of the Indian media at large. With Naresh Rajput who owned the major national and regional level media channels behind the bars, it became far more evident that how they manufactured news and influenced the mindset of the common people. She became a household name. She continued her quest for more far reaching influential investigative journalism delving deep into it every time she got any feed. Her viewership was breaking records every day. And, so her offers for job. She was even offered humongous sum to join an international media firm starting up in India. But she didn't accept it. She wanted to work independently and kept her obligation to herself only. She decided to start a news agency on her own but she had time for it. It was too early for her to do something of that scale.

On the seventh day of her term as the Chief Minister of Maharashtra, Shreya Basu decided to pay a visit to the Arthur Road Jail where they were kept till the case would go the court. The visit had to be done on a very secretive manner without the knowledge of media or for that matter any party members. The jailer was intimated on the urgency of the visit.

As they went inside the cell where Naresh Rajput was kept, she could see his eyes raging like a bull as he looked at them. "Hope you're enjoying your days here." Shreya quipped at him. "You may call me Ms. Chief Minister as you might know already I have been officially appointed as the one."

Naresh Rajput hissed into her ears like snake spitting venom, "I would be outside the jail before you take the first meal tomorrow. Just wait for me outside the court."

"I know. In fact, I too want that. *Outside the jail.* I want to have my next meal in complete peace." Shreya told as she was walking out.

The next morning was again a day of media frenzy. The seven people among whom there were people like ex-CM Manoj Pawar and media tycoon

Naresh Rajput would be taken to court. High protection was allotted. People rallied across the state for their punishment. The youths across the state marched towards Mumbai High Court demanding their lifelong sentence. Debates were held across various news spaces on their punishment range.

Shreya Basu was at her office, sipping rare aromatic Oolong tea from the transparent cup with Malik sitting across her in a chair. She could hear people cheering her name outside. *This is the best feeling. When people cheer your name and applaud you for something they have loved, it overshadows the guilt of being wrong,* she wondered. *May be this is the magic of power. Of being powerful.*

Taking his eyes off the files piled before him, Malik asked, "They will be bailed out today itself. Once out, he would be after us." In her impeccable style, she snapped sharp at him with a steel smile. "Things are taken care of."

The afternoon news channels were abuzz with a deadly accident near circle of Haji Ali Dargah at Mahalaxmi. As the witnesses told the media they saw the police vehicle being road-blocked by a huge truck near the circle and they broke open the vehicle to rescue the prisoners from the vehicle. The guarding police shot fire at them, but they defended them with rifles with incessant firings openly. The prisoners escaped in a van. And the people who came for rescue went away in a separate car in a separate direction. The prisoners speeded the car across the road which incidentally brake-failed and crashed resulting in death of all three of them. Fortunately, only two police officers were only hit by a bullet on their arms. They were readily taken to hospital and treated immediately.

The incident resulted in a surprise among the residents. They readily termed it as a result of their *Karma. It's the rage of the Gods that it happened. They were punished for their crime,* a person told as a reaction to the incident.

Though some curious noses smelled fish, Shreya Basu took things on her stride at an evening press meet stating. "We are deeply saddened by the death of Mr. Naresh Rajput, Mahesh Shinde and Manoj Pawar. Though they were accused of some serious offences, I always believe in right to trial. We will definitely equip our police to face such issues from now. Our heartfelt condolences to their families and closed ones…"

The politician she has become, Malik thought and smiled within as he heard Shreya speaking to the media.

The movement in Balochistan, though got momentum for a while under Ghalib Alam, was ruthlessly crushed by the army of the federal government. Huge number of arms and weapons which were supposed to be used by the rebels were allegedly seized by the federal force.

Hundreds of Baloch people involved in the movement were arrested and put behind the bars. The movement was completely halted. As a symbolic victory against the rebels, the federal government built a special task office to keep an intense eye on the region.

The special task force, an arm of Pakistan intelligence agency, had been successful in keeping things on check. But they were in search of two people, a male and a female, who according to their intelligence sources were planning for re-igniting the revolution. Despite several sources, they were unable to catch them. Each of their attempts was cleverly triumphed by the duo's clever acts. Apart from the information of the lady being involved in a bank heist and the guy being involved in a pick-pocket racket, no information was available on them. The duo, namely Soha Zarnaaz and Farhan Awuza, were looking for the right moment to strike back.

Ziro was a nice place to be. Away from all the prosaic things, amongst the lush greenery and abundance of oxygen around, Hector at last found what he was looking for a long time. Peace. The quaint old town in the lap of nature was an escape.

Far from all acquaintances of reality, Hector was finding life among the Pine Hills and tribal people living there. He lived in a small hut and helped people grow paddy in fields. One day as he returned from the fields, he was startled as he was greeted in his own house by lanky person.

"Welcome home, champ." Kuldeep Singh extended his hand for a shake. "Hope you have had enough of a vacation here." He looked around and lauded his small hut.

"Well, let's talk business then."

Sankha Ghosh is a banker by day and writer by night. Starting off as an environmental activist with an international foundation, he eventually got into the exciting industry of banking. An avid observer, an alternate thinker, and strictly opinionated, his writings have been published in several national and international blogs.